COINED BY GOD

Also by Stanley Malless and Jeffrey McQuain

COINED BY SHAKESPEARE

THE ELEMENTS OF ENGLISH

COINED BY GOD

WORDS AND PHRASES

THAT FIRST APPEAR IN

THE ENGLISH TRANSLATIONS

OF THE BIBLE

Stanley Malless & Jeffrey McQuain

W. W. Norton & Company
New York London

Manufacturing by Quebecor Fairfield
Book design by Blue Shoe Studio
Production manager: Julia Druskin

LIBRARY OF CONGRESS CATALOGING-IN-PUBLICATION DATA

Malless, Stan, 1947–
Coined by God : words and phrases that first appear in the English
translations of the Bible / Stanley Malless and Jeffrey McQuain.
p. cm.
Includes bibliographical references and indexes.
ISBN 0-393-02045-2
1. Bible. English—Versions—History. 2. English language—New words.
3. Bible—Language, style. I. McQuain, Jeff, 1955– . II. Title.
BS455.M33 2003
428.1—dc21

2002013332

W. W. Norton & Company, Inc., 500 Fifth Avenue, New York, N.Y. 10110
www.wwnorton.com

W. W. Norton & Company Ltd., Castle House, 75/76 Wells Street,
London W1T 3QT

1 2 3 4 5 6 7 8 9 0

TO JANIE LASCH,

WHOSE BIBLE HAS ALWAYS BEEN THE BOOK OF LOVE

—S.M.

IN LOVING MEMORY OF MY PARENTS,

WHO FIRST SHARED WITH ME THE GOOD BOOK

—J.M.

CONTENTS

ACNOWLEDGMENTS

If we were to thank everything and everyone that helped to make this book possible, we'd have another Book of Kings (and Queens) on our hands. Our hope is for at least a Book of Psalms.

In the beginning were our sources: *Merriam-Webster's Collegiate Dictionary Deluxe Electronic Edition* provided the raw list of those words that first appeared in English on or near the year of publication of key translations of the Bible; the *Oxford English Dictionary Online* (a godsend of an innovation) verified those words as biblical coinages and also led us to the phrases that were "coined by God"; the masterful scholarship (and accessibility) of the Forshall/Madden 1982 reprint edition of Wycliffe's Bible; David Daniell's recent editions of Tyndale's 1534 modern-spelling edition of Tyndale's revised 1526 New Testament (1989) and the 1530 Pentateuch (1992); the very recent (1998) Lazarus Ministry Press reprint of the Geneva Bible; Oxford's World's Classics Edition (Carroll and Prickett, eds.) of the King James Version with Apocrypha (1997); and the University of Chicago's ARTFL Project: Multi-Lingual Bibles (www.lib.uchicago.edu/efts/ARTFL/public/bibles/), all made cross-referencing a pleasure.

But if we have sources but not family, friends, and colleagues, we are nothing.

Dr. Malless extends his deepest gratitude to his mother, Norine Wolf Malless, for her lifelong study of the English biblical tradition and for a love of liberty that she learned from Wycliffe, Tyndale, and Luther. Other family members who've provided support, inspiration, and comic relief are Dee and Paul Kovary, Karen and Joe Leckemby, Alison and Peter Kvetko, and Dawn Baker. Near-family members include Bob DeGiorgio and Bob Hagins. Among the faculty and staff at Simpson College, whose skill, expertise, and professionalism cleared the way to a happy ending, are the following: Cyd Dyer, director of Simpson's Dunn Library, who put all of the abovementioned resources either in his hands or at his fingertips; interlibrary loan magician Kristi Ellingson for her Wycliffite patience; Dr. Jackie Crawford, for being such an understanding department chair (for the second time); Kathy Witzenburg, whose superb editorial assistance and word processing skills have been indispensable; and professors Robert Gieber and Patricia Calkins for their help with Jerome's Latin and Luther's German, respectively. Also a very very special thanks to his coauthor, Jeffrey McQuain, on this, their twenty-fifth anniversary of friendship and professional collaboration. Finally, a life's worth of loving gratitude to his wife, professor of social work and chair of the Department of Social Science at Simpson College, Jane Lasch Kvetko, to whom he dedicates this book.

Returning the warm salute to his coauthor for the genesis of this idea, Dr. McQuain wishes to express special thanks to his brother, Dan, for his computer expertise. Among others who have offered support and assistance are June Carson;

Marguerite Coley; Ruth and Lois Dolly; Dr. Charlotte Fallenius; Professor Robert Feldman; Lynda Foro, director of Foro for Animals; Hank Gant; Lynn Lawrence Hanson; Julie Harris; Jeffrey D. Jones; Lynn Karpen; Mildred Kline; Steven and Susan Koppe; Chris McMurry; Virginia and Robert McQuain; Kathleen Miller; the congregation of North Bethesda United Methodist Church in Maryland; Professor Barbara Stout of Montgomery College (Md.); Dr. H. Byrd Teter; Mary Tonkinson; Dr. Leonard Wisneski; Ann Rubin Wort; and especially Professor Thomas Cannon Jr. of the American University's Department of Literature.

In addition, both authors offer deep gratitude to David Hendin, our agent; to William Safire for his inspirational words about words; and to Amy Cherry, our editor at W. W. Norton.

INTRODUCTION

. . . AND SWEET RELIGION MAKES
A RHAPSODY OF WORDS.
    —Shakespeare, *Hamlet* (III.iv.47–48)

IN THE BEGINNING WAS THE WORD, AND THE WORD
WAS WITH GOD, AND THE WORD WAS GOD.
    —John 1:1 (King James translation of the Bible)

Members of the clergy enjoy telling the story of the "old school" parishioner who, upon hearing of a new American Authorized Version of the Bible, snipped that "If the King James Version was good enough for St. Paul, it's good enough for me." English, of course, was not the first language of the Bible. The New Testament of St. Paul's day was written in *koine* ("common") Greek, and the original Old Testament was almost entirely written in Hebrew, with minor passages in Aramaic (which was later to be the language of Jesus of Nazareth). The word *Bible*, in fact, is not native to the English language. It comes from the Greek word for "book" (*biblos*).

Inspired to find the eternally right words, the earliest translators of the Bible into English had assimilated a 1,500-year history of Biblical translations by studying Biblical paraphrases and glosses that had been written in Old English, and by relying on their own uneven knowledge of the Hebrew,

Greek, and Latin languages. And it is this seemingly unstoppable *tradition* of Biblical translation and interpretation that we are calling "God" in our title, *Coined by God*. The 131 entries that we've included represent only a fraction of the words, phrases, rhythms, and idioms that have entered the English language as a result of biblical translations. Except for some of the phrase variations, these entries have no earlier recorded history in written or printed English, although the terms may have already existed in common (*koine*) English usage. Other than its lexical identity as a first-timer, however, for a word or phrase to be *Coined by God*, it had to meet one simple criterion: appear for the first time in a complete English translation of the Old Testament, the New Testament, or both. Excluded were the many partial Old English translations of psalms, gospels, and individual books of the Bible. This meant that we bookended our range of possibilities, on the one hand, between the first English translation of the complete Bible (1382) by John Wycliffe and his followers and, on the other, the six "companies" (committees) responsible for the King James Version (1611). It also became evident to us that this symmetry held literary as well as political significance: Wycliffe (c. 1330–1384) was a contemporary of Chaucer (c. 1342–1400), and both shared the patronage of John of Gaunt; the King James translators, active between 1604 and 1611, were contemporaries of William Shakespeare, and all enjoyed the support of King James I. Between these testaments to the English language, other versions of the English Bible evolved, but of those translations the Tyndale (1526 and 1534 New Testaments and the 1530 Pentateuch), Coverdale (1535), and

Geneva (1560) Bibles proved to be the main sources of new English words and phrases.

From a God's-eye view, however, English came late onto the biblical scene. The earliest Hebrew Scripture was in use about 1000 B.C., and by 500 B.C. much of the Torah had been translated into Aramaic, the common language spoken by Jews at that time throughout the Middle East. The first Greek version of the Hebrew, the Septuagint, was completed about 250 B.C., and the first Christian New Testament appeared in Greek about A.D. 350, which was, in turn, translated into another vernacular, Latin, leading to St. Jerome's Vulgate of the fifth century. (Of the other versions of Scripture current in his day, Jerome was reported to have said that they were "not versions but *sub*versions.") By the ninth century A.D., partial translations (and prose glosses) of the Bible into Anglo-Saxon (Old English) were appearing in manuscripts such as the *Vespasian Psalter*, which is a Latin translation of the Book of Psalms with a literal translation in Anglo-Saxon written above the Latin. Similarly, the earliest English version of the New Testament, the *Lindisfarne Gospels* manuscript, appeared about the tenth century in the same interlinear Latin/Anglo-Saxon format. But it was not until 1382–88 and the Middle English of Chaucer's time that John Wycliffe and his followers completed a full translation of the entire Bible into the common English of *that* day. If in the beginning was the Word, then in the end, the operative word for the common-sense history of biblical translation must surely be "*koine*ages."

Even the names of the biblical books, from Genesis and Exodus to Revelation, have enlarged the vocabulary of

English. These Bible words, beginning with every letter but *x*, each contain a story, a wealth of learning and experience too often forgotten in contemporary usage. Consider the "treasure" (another Wycliffe coinage) within *shibboleth*. In the Old Testament, the Book of Judges contains the earliest of spy stories: When the conquered Ephraimites try to escape by passing themselves off as the conquering Gileadites, the pretenders are asked to pronounce the Gileadite word *shibboleth* ("an ear of corn"), but because of their language idiosyncrasies, they can produce only the mispronunciation "sibboleth." In this case it was a dead giveaway, and they were summarily executed. Today the English use of *shibboleth* for a code word or telling example of insider jargon has moved far beyond its biblical origin. Newcomers to the nation's capital, for instance, can be readily identified by the "shibboleth" of "Silver Spring," a suburb of Washington often mispronounced as a plural, "Silver Springs."

Not only did hundreds of individual words first appear in English when biblical translators used them, but so did dozens of common phrases, from *apple of his eye* and *two-edged sword*, to *salt of the earth*. Some, however, like the allusive *good Samaritan*, *promised land*, and *old wives' tales*, are clearly biblical in origin, but they do not appear in the Bible verbatim. Thus they are not "coined by God" as our criterion requires.

Finally, from *appetite* to *cucumber*, from *exorcist* to *wrinkle*, our book offers edifying entries about word trajectories—that secular words can become biblical and, in turn, that biblical words can become secular. But the entries also show *how* words have come into our language—from the functional shifting of nouns (*brain* as a verb), the compounding of shorter words (*busybody*), the direct borrowing of a word from its non-English text (*glory* from the Latin *gloria*), and the appropriation of proper names, giving us *Sodom and Gomorrah* and the *land of Nod*. Also included is a brief chronology of the English Bible in translation as well as separate indexes by entry, by translator, and by books of the Bible. Reader-friendly regardless of the reader's faith, our book will reward you with a greater understanding of the English language, of the Bible, and of our culture—through words, as it were, coined by God.

ADOPTION

(noun) the act of voluntarily taking up into any relation

Long before college professors missed their campus bookstore deadlines for textbook **adoptions**, **adoption** originally appeared in the first English Bible in Romans 8:23, where Paul/Wycliffe says, "We . . . sorrow within us for the **adoption** of God's son." Adopted by nearly every subsequent translator since then, the noun appears only five times in Wycliffe's Bible—as a cluster in Paul's Letters to the Romans, Ephesians, and Galatians.

Ironically, this type of coinage is what the philologists call an "adoption" or "the taking of a word belonging to a foreign language into regular use in [one's] own, without (intentional) change of form" (*OED*). In this case, the crossover word is the Latin *adoptionem*, as found in the Latin Bible or Vulgate from which Wycliffe was translating. A combination of the Latin roots *ad* ("to") and *optare* ("to choose"), **adoption** literally means "to opt for" and is derived from the same root that gives us another choice word, *option*.

Nowadays the staying power of the noun **adoption** is evident in its functional shift to the adjectival form—most commonly found in the early-twentieth-century coinage "**adoption** agency." Recently, however, as a result of the contentious partisan politics of the last several years, the adjective's reach has been extended to the nation—*Adoption Nation: How the Adoption Revolution Is Transforming America* by Adam Pertman, published in 2000.

AfFINITY

(noun) relationship or kinship generally between individuals or races

Wycliffe uses this noun for the first time in the Book of Ruth when Boaz advises Ruth that there is another man who is "nigher than I" in kinship and therefore has the prior claim of marriage. He says, "If he will take thee by right of **affinity** the thing is well do" (3:13). But this initial usage was short-lived. In Tyndale's version, for example, **affinity** shifts to the specific relationship of *marriage*: "if he will marry thee it is good, so let him do." By the time of King James, the passage returns to the kinship relationship, but now the Latin word **affinity** is replaced by the Old English root *cynn*: "if he will perform unto thee the part of a kinsman, well; let him do the kinsman's part."

From the Latin *affinis*, which is a combination of the root *ad* ("to") and *finis* ("border" or "limit"), in current usage **affinity** has developed an **affinity** as an adjective for everything from biochemistry, "**affinity** chromatography," to banking, "**affinity** credit card" (so called because to get one, membership is required in an **affinity** group or association). Considering that *finis* is also the source of *final* and *finish* (and its etymologically redundant expression *finish line*), the lineage of an **affinity** card depends entirely upon its credit line.

Af f LICTION

(noun) a condition of great physical or mental pain or distress

Jehovah coins this long-suffering noun in Wycliffe's version of Exodus 3:7, where appearing as the burning bush, He reveals to Moses that "I have seen the **affliction** of my people in Egypt." Derived from the Latin prefix *ad* ("to") plus the root *figere* ("to strike or beat against"), the verb form *afflict* is often mistaken for its sibling, *inflict*, which stems from the same Latin root. (The difference between the two is primarily in the grammatical construction, e.g., someone *inflicts* suffering on another person, but the community was *afflicted* with a scandal.)

Although Tyndale translates **affliction** as "trouble" ("I have surely seen the trouble of my people"), the King James Version and its revisions return to the original word, which, in addition to its variants (*afflict*, *afflicted*), is found in over a hundred passages throughout the Bible. Shakespeare, by comparison, used it half as many times, most memorably, perhaps, when Friar Laurence tells the love-sick Romeo that "**Affliction** is enamor'd of thy parts, / And thou art wedded to calamity" (III.iii.3–4). By the nineteenth century, however, Jane Austen had "civilized" the pain of **affliction** in her novel *Mansfield Park*, where she observed, "So harmonised by distance . . . every former **affliction** had its charm." But by the end of the last millennium, *Affliction*, the 1998 movie starring Nick Nolte, returned it to the uncivilized side of human nature. As a reviewer in the *Boston Globe* put it: "The **affliction** in *Affliction* is the chain of emotional barrenness and eruptive violence passed from father to son in a bleak and metaphorically wintry New Hampshire town."

ALLEGORY

(noun) the representation of one thing (in which key elements—e.g., characters, etc.—are given deeper meaning) in terms of other things of aptly suggestive resemblance

In Paul's Letter to the Galatians, Wycliffe uses **allegory** for the first time in English. Telling his audience that he is "perplexed" over their insistence on following Mosaic law over Christian faith, Paul reminds them that language often portrays things in the guise of something else. Specifically, he refers to the story of Hagar and Sarah as "[That] which [has] been said by **allegory**, or ghostly understanding" (4:24).

In the Latin of the Vulgate, the word appears as *allegoriam*, Jerome's transliteration of the original Greek, *allegoria*. In like manner, Wycliffe also adopts the word exactly as it is written, minus the inflectional ending. Tyndale, however, avoids it altogether and translates the passage as "Which things betoken mystery." (The King James translators keep Tyndale's phrase but reenlist **allegory** as a replacement for "mystery.")

A combination of the Greek roots *allos* ("other") and *agora* ("speaking," with the added nuance of *agora*, "the public assembly"), **allegory** occurs only this one time in the Bible. Nonetheless, from Keats's observation in a letter to his brother (1819) that a "man's life of any worth is a continual **allegory**," to the bedevilment of students in high school English class, to the "mysteries" of postmodernism's "**allegories** of reading," **allegory** has sustained a long history of "otherspeak."

ALL THINGS TO ALL MEN
universality; ability to satisfy everybody

This expression comes from the translation of Paul's First Letter to the church at Corinth. In making every conceivable effort to gain converts to Christianity, Paul professes that "unto the Jews I became a Jew" and "To the weak became I as weak." Attempting to be universally accepted, Paul writes, "I am made **all things to all men**, that I might by all means save some" (1 Corinthians 9:22).

At least, that's the word order in the 1611 King James Version of Paul's epistle. Two centuries earlier, John Wycliffe's translation has "To all men I am made all things." The phrase uses "all" twice, but that three-letter word hardly makes this phrase unique in the Bible: a concordance by James Strong provides sixteen pages of biblical entries that include "all," ranging from "over all the earth" in Genesis to "be with you all" in Revelation.

In modern times, the humorist P. G. Wodehouse used Paul's expression in *Quick Service* (1940) to comment that "it is of the essence of a barmaid's duties that she be **all things to**

all men." As if the possibility of being **all things to all men** were not difficult enough, the phrase has been stretched even further nowadays in order to become gender-neutral as "all things to all people." Christine S. Ammer, in her *American Heritage Dictionary of Idioms* (1997), noted its current use in negative terms: "Today it often appears in a political context, but phrased negatively, as in 'He wants to be a good school committee member, but he can't be all things to all people.' "

ALPHA AND OMEGA

first and last; the range of all things

Not until the final book of the Bible does this phrase make its first appearance. Readers of Revelation, however, will find these words used four times in its chapters, including, appropriately, the first and the last.

The all encompassing term **alpha and omega** links the first and final letters of the Greek alphabet (in fact, our English word *alphabet* begins with the first Greek letter, *alpha*, joined to the start of the second letter, *beta*). In the Wycliffe translation of 1382, the letters are expressed as "alpha and oo," but it is translated by Tyndale in 1526 as **alpha and omega**. As was generally the case, the King James Version followed Tyndale's lead: "I am the **alpha and omega**, the beginning and the ending, saith the Lord, which is, and which was, and which is to come, the Almighty" (Revelation 1:9).

Alpha is adapted from *aleph*, the first letter of the Phoenician alphabet and originally the hieroglyph of an ox's

7

head (α). From that ancient beginning, the word has soared into outer space, from the Alpha space station to Alpha Centauri, the triple star closest to our sun. Even the regular activity of the human brain is measured in "alpha waves." The equally ancient *omega* is the twenty-fourth and final Greek letter (Ω). It comes from the phrase *o mega*, meaning "large 'o'" (for a long vowel), with *mega* still used as a prefix for "large" or "many," as in *megabytes*. Scientists have embraced this Greek letter as well, from Omega Centauri, a globular cluster in space, to omega-3, a type of polyunsaturated fatty acid found mostly in fish or vegetables.

Indicating infinity, the combination of **alpha and omega** (both usually capitalized) was celebrated in the nineteenth-century hymn "Love Divine, All Loves Excelling," extolling God as "**Alpha and Omega** be." Applied outside religion by the British astronomer Sir John Herschel in 1830 to "the **alpha and omega** of science," the lowercased words were poetically extended by Thomas Carlyle, the Scottish historian, in writing about Frederick the Great. "This Siege of Dresden," Carlyle commented in his 1865 biography of the king of Prussia, "is the alpha to whatever omegas there may be." Less lofty, perhaps, is today's use of the phrase by a Florida company known as **Alpha and Omega** Pest Control.

AMBITIOUS

(adjective) strongly in pursuit of honor or advancement; aspiring to high position

Some two hundred years before Shakespeare penned Mark Antony's classic funeral oration and its brutally sarcastic refrain of "Brutus says he [Caesar] was **ambitious** / and Brutus is an honorable man" (*Julius Caesar*, III.ii.93–94), Wycliffe debuts this power adjective in Paul's First Letter to the Corinthians. Unlike Mark Antony, who aspires to stir the crowd to revolt against the new regime, Paul hopes to inspire a revolution of love in the faithful of Corinth. In a key passage of what has been called his "Hymn on Christian Love," he stresses what love is *not*: "Not inblown . . . not **ambitious** or covetous of worship" (13:5).

A direct adoption from the Vulgate *ambitiosa*, **ambitious** and its then contemporary noun coinage *ambition* are rooted in the Latin *ambitio*, meaning "a going around" (probably in the sense of soliciting votes), a connotation evident in the related sixteenth-century words *ambit* and *ambient*. Although **ambitious** never appears again in the English translations of the Bible, it has had a long and varied career in the English language, denoting everything from a finger (Shakespeare's "No man's pie is freed / From his **ambitious** finger" [*Henry VIII*, I.i.52–53]) to the latest Jim Henson Interactive cartoon (" 'The Kermambo' is the most **ambitious** MuppeToon© created thus far by our team").

ANCIENT OF DAYS

the Almighty; one of advanced age

Different translators choose different words to express the same concept. *Ancient*, for example, is not the first English word selected for this expression in the Book of Daniel. Wycliffe uses "elde," and Coverdale prefers "old-aged." But it is the Geneva Bible of 1560 that introduces **Ancient of Days** ("Ancient of daies"), the phrase that has withstood the test of time.

Daniel speaks these words in the King James Version after he falls asleep and has an apocalyptic dream. Of this fantastic vision, he reports, "I beheld till the thrones were cast down, and the **Ancient of Days** did sit" (Daniel 7:9). Daniel describes the Ancient as one whose "garment was white as snow, and the hair of his head like the pure wool; his throne was like the fiery flame, and his wheels as burning fire."

As a noun, *ancient* (originally an adjective) had barely entered the English language in the sixteenth century, and it was used most often for "old man" or "one who lived in ancient times." The word caught on, however, as a biblical term, capitalized when used for the Almighty. In 1830, Robert Grant included that phrase in his lyrics for the hymn "O, Worship the King," rhapsodizing about "our shield and defender—the **Ancient of Days**, / Pavilioned in splendor and girded with praise."

Beyond the religious use, though, have come whimsical applications of the phrase to old people or things. T. E. Lawrence, for instance, used the phrase facetiously in a 1935 letter mentioning his motorcycle: "I've only ridden the

ancient-of-days twice this year." Later that year, Lawrence was killed in a motorcycle accident.

APPETITE

(noun) inclination toward the attainment of an object or a purpose; desire, tendency, disposition

Although **appetite** as the desire for food predates Wycliffe's coinage by seventy years, and Chaucer's use of it for the first time to denote a *capacity* for food comes fifteen years afterward, Wycliffe's usage in Ezekiel is the first time the noun refers to desire in general. (No subsequent English version uses **appetite** in translating this passage.) In Wycliffe's Ezekiel the noun occurs in the oracular words of Jehovah as they are spoken by the prophet: "go thou to the right, or to the left, whither ever is the **appetite** or desire of thy face" (21:16).

Taken directly from the Latin Bible, **appetite** derives from *appetitus* ("eager desire for"), which is composed of the roots *ad* ("to") and *petere* ("to fall, rush at, seek"). The latter is also at the root of *petition* and the suffixlike term *petal* that forms the "falling toward" adjective *centripetal*. Later translators moved **appetite** away from Wycliffe's solo usage, opting instead for other verses and chapters. Of the four passages that survived into the revised versions, the most familiar, perhaps, is the King James phrase "a man given to **appetite**" (Proverbs 23:2).

But for each of the four biblical turns of phrase, thousands of **appetites** claim their place in the written language.

Wordsworth, for instance, gave it a new inner dimension when, in "Lines Composed a Few Miles above Tintern Abbey," he reminisced that "the colours" and the "forms" of "the tall rock, / The mountain, and the deep and gloomy wood, / . . . were then to me / An **appetite**; a feeling and a love." H. L. Mencken, however, in not such a lyrical mood in *A Book of Prefaces* (1917), criticized "The virulence of the national **appetite** for bogus revelation." And in a recent *Los Angeles Times* assessment of Adam Sandler's acting ability, the reviewer identified "the bedrock of [Sandler's] success" as "an uncanny aptitude for pandering to gross-out **appetites** of teenage boys."

APPLE OF HIS EYE

favorite or well-liked object of another's affections

Not every biblical phrase has come into English directly from the Bible. An indirect coinage, for instance, is **apple of his eye**, which appears five times in the Old Testament. Tyndale offers it first in translating the words that Moses speaks about God's connection to the patriarch Jacob: "he led him about, and gave him understanding, and kept him as the **apple of his eye**" (Deuteronomy 32:10). Five years later, Coverdale's 1535 Bible uses the expression in translating Zechariah, who reminds the Children of Zion that they are the Lord's chosen people: "Who so toucheth you, shall touch the **apple of his eye**" (Zechariah 2:8).

Hundreds of years before that, though, the phrase was

already introduced into Old English by King Aelfred. In the ninth century, he translated "Gregory's Pastoral Rule," a guide for church government, and turned the Latin phrase into English. Eight centuries later, the poet John Milton identified the apple as the fruit of Adam and Eve's downfall. Although the human anatomy does include a throat projection known as an *Adam's apple*, the original fruit (*bad*, in Hebrew) in the Garden of Eden was generic. The King James translation of the Book of Genesis refers only to "fruit," without specifying "apple," much less "Red Delicious" or "Grimes Golden."

So how did it become the fruit of favoritism in human vision? This "apple" refers to the pupil of the eye, once believed to be a solid round body. Writers from Shakespeare to Sir Walter Scott picked up on this ancient belief that the eye's center was solid like an apple. Modern writers, though, have tended to ridicule the image, including the poet Roy Campbell's 1930 questioning in "11" of "The apple, nay the onion, of his eye?" In place of those saucy words, though, we prefer the sweeter imagery of a 1586 poet who reminds us that "We see our own eyes shine within the apples of our neighbors' eyes."

ARGUMENT

(noun) the presenting of evidence; proof, manifestation

In Acts 1:3 Wycliffe is the first to use **argument** as a synonym for "clear evidence." Speaking to "Theophilus," the author of Acts begins his narrative by tracing the history of the Christian movement, starting with the resurrection of Jesus; it is in that context that he emphasizes the various proofs or **arguments** for Jesus' appearance after his crucifixion: "To which and he showed himself alive, or quick, after his passion, in many **arguments** or provings." Subsequent English translations of this passage avoid **argument** in favor of "token" (Tyndale) and "proofs" (King James and Revised). In fact, only two citations survive in the modern revisions: "arguments" and "arguing," both in the Book of Job.

Although the more familiar meaning of "a statement advanced for the purpose of influencing the mind" appears in Chaucer a mere four years after Wycliffe's coinage, **argument** in both senses of "clarity" (revelation and purposefulness) originates in the Indo-European base *ar(e)g* ("gleaming" or "whitish"). This same root forms the Latin word for "silver," *argentum* ("Ag" in the periodic table), and thus by association the silver lining of the unconcealment or shining forth of an **argument**.

Today no one would argue against **argument** being a mother lode of meaning for the English language. Beyond the familiar uses in philosophy, law, and logic, examples pop up in mathematics (an **argument** is an independent variable of a function), linguistics (a noun element in a clause), and as noun and adjective in the language of computer science ("to connect a segment search **argument** with the next **argument** list in the . . . search field list" [*Computerworld*, March 1984]).

B

BALD HEAD

(noun) the condition of having little or no hair on the head; someone who has this condition

Although this noun is attributed to Miles Coverdale and his 1535 translation of the complete Bible, scholars argue for Tyndale's authorship of several of the books in Coverdale's Old Testament, including 2 Kings, where **bald head** appears for the first time in written English. There, having just succeeded his master Elijah as religious leader, the prophet Elisha is on route to Bethel when he is confronted by a group of boys from the city. With name-calling mockery they taunt him to "Come up here thou **balde heade**" (2:23).

The origin of the adjective *bald* is uncertain, but it probably comes from an ancestral root *bal*, denoting "shiny" or "white spot" (as in **baldheaded** eagle). As an adjective, it modifies "head" in a dozen passages throughout the Bible—mostly in Leviticus in the context of diagnosing leprous spots on the head; however, **bald head** as a noun only appears this one time in the Bible.

Since Elisha's humiliating experience on the road to Bethel, a new iconography has grown up around the **bald head**. From the vacation resort on **Bald Head** Island, North Carolina, to the venerable Mr. Clean (and his offspring Jesse Ventura), the polished image of the **bald head** now is celebrated around the world. As a reporter for the *Ottawa Citizen* explained on the occasion of Mr. Clean's fortieth birthday: "With his **bald head** and earring, he certainly looks more comfortable in the 90s than he did when he was first invented by a Chicago advertising agency in 1959."

BALM IN GILEAD

healing ointment; cure-all

"Is there no **balm in Gilead**; is there no physician there?" the Lord asks rhetorically in the King James Version of Jeremiah 8:22. "Why then is not the health of the daughter of my people recovered?"

The answer, of course, is that Gilead was already long known for its balm. This healing product is mentioned as early as the Old Testament story of Joseph's **coat of many colors** (see entry), when a company of traders arrives "from Gilead bearing spicery and balm" (Genesis 37:25). In fact, some versions of the Bible have become famous just for the way they chose to translate this phrase. A 1568 version was known as the Treacle Bible for asking, "Is there no tryacle in Gilead?" In 1609, another translation used "rosin," making that version the Rosin Bible. More recent versions have substituted the word "medicine." However, the King James Version was the first to introduce the phrase into the written language. (Wycliffe chose "gomme" and "resyn," Coverdale introduced "balm," but the King James translators changed the preposition from "Balm *at* Gilead" to **balm in Gilead**.)

From Jerome's Latin noun *balsamum* ("balsum"), which translates the Hebrew *basam*, this curative has been described as a fragrant golden gum, probably from a small evergreen tree

17

(*commiphora opobalsamum*) cultivated to help in healing wounds or soothing pain. When healing did not occur, however, *balm* was also the term for perfume used to help em*balm* the dead. Other terms for a healing ointment include *balm of Mecca* and the *American Balm of Gilead*.

Although the phrase has been known for its use in a folk hymn ("There is a **balm in Gilead** to make the wounded whole, / There is a **balm in Gilead** to heal the sin-sick soul"), most recently a New York–based nonprofit organization that works with African American churches in the fight against AIDS has taken **Balm in Gilead** as its name.

BEAUTIfUL

(adjective) excelling in grace of form and other qualities that are very pleasing to the eye

In the twenty-third chapter of Tyndale's Matthew, Jesus challenges the gathered crowd to abandon rabbinic law. Powered by the refrain "Woe be to you scribes and Pharisees, hypocrites!" his exhortation moves through a series of metaphors, each one developing the theme of non-Christian pretense. Perhaps the most memorable of these metaphors compares the hypocrites to "painted tombs which appear **beautiful** outward: but are within full of dead bones and of all filthiness" (23:27). This is the first time that **beautiful** appears in English. (The earlier Wycliffe chose "faire.")

From the Latin *bellus*, "pretty" or "lovely," and its Old French descendant, *Beltat* (which gave them *beauté* and us

18

beauty), plus the suffix *ful*, **beautiful** ultimately shows up in dozens of passages throughout the King James and the Revised Versions of the Bible—but only half as many times as its noun-sibling, *beauty*.

These days **beautiful** has become so commonplace that it has nearly assumed the status of an American cliché. We find it in song titles ("America the **Beautiful**," "**Beautiful** Dreamer," "Oh, What a **Beautiful** Mornin'"), in political slogans ("Black is **beautiful**"), in socio-economic class distinctions ("**beautiful** people"), in book titles (*Small Is Beautiful*, *All Things Bright and Beautiful*), in movie titles (Sally Field's recent directorial debut, *Beautiful*), and even as a fashion statement where sense becomes scents (Estée Lauder's new promo perfume, **Beautiful**).

BLAB

(verb) to give away a secret in idle talk; to talk much and ineptly

Coverdale first records this gossipy verb in his version of Proverbs: "A foolish mouth **blabbeth** out nothinge but fool-ishnesse" (15:2). Unique to this one passage in the Bible, the verb has been silenced in all other English translations. The earlier Wycliffe, for instance, opts for "boileth out folly," and the nearly contemporary Geneva favors a distant cousin, "bab-bleth." However, a generation later the King James translators select "poureth out foolishness," which is then modernized by the Revised Versionists as "pour out folly."

Ironically, to speculate on the origins of **blab** is to define the verb itself, for hard evidence is virtually nonexistent. Apparently it shares some family ties with the Old Norse *blabbra* (probably onomatopoeic) and the Old Dutch *labben* ("to chatter"), but its echoic quality also can be heard in *babble*, *blather*, *gab*, and possibly in the expression *blah, blah, blah*. Several generations before Coverdale, in fact, Chaucer used *labbe* as a noun—and synonym for **blab** (*Troilus and Criseyde*, III.301).

But in spite of its questionable background, **blab** has successfully **blabbed** itself into the digital age. A recent headline in *Business Wire*, for example, read, "**Blab**Studios.com Becomes Latest Division of **Blab**Media, Inc." And a catchy advertisement bragged, "**Blab** for free: Internet telephony will soon reduce the cost of long-distance calls to nothing." Even instructional technology is spoken for with the marketing of a video series designed to help children learn language. The program's title? "Blip and **Blab**."

BLIND LEAD THE BLIND
ineffectual or limited assistance

In Tyndale's version, scribes and Pharisees of Jerusalem question Jesus about the breaking of religious traditions. His answers offend them: "Let them alone," he tells his disciples, "they be the blind leaders of the blind. If the **blind lead the blind**, both shall fall into the ditch" (Matthew 15:14). This mid-sixteenth-century coinage was adopted by subsequent translators, and by the seventeenth century, the wording evolved into the **blind leading the blind** as a commentary on poor or inept leadership.

Although considered by some to be derogatory toward the visually challenged, the expression is still widely used today, especially in variations. At a recent Modern Language Association convention, one of the scheduled papers offered as its title, "Who Is Leading Whom? Teaching German to Students Who Are Blind." Wordplay on the phrase has also produced *Blind Leading the Naked*, a 1986 alternative rock album by Violent Femmes. Other variations include "the bland leading the bland" and even "the blond leading the blond."

BLOOD MONEY

(noun) money gotten at the expense of others' lives or suffering

The Bible is a book of bloodlines and blood-words. Hundreds of passages include either the word *blood* or a compound with *blood* as its base. **Blood money** is one of those compounds, and it turns up for the first time in English by way of Coverdale's translation of the twenty-seventh chapter of Matthew: Troubled by what to do with the thirty pieces of silver that Judas has returned to them, the priests decide that "It is not lawful to put them into the Gods chest for it is **blood-money**" (27:6).

Coverdale also coins another blood-word, **bloodthirsty**, which appears in the Book of Psalms: "O destroy not my soul with the sinners, nor my life with the **bloodthirsty**" (25:9). The source of each word, however, is in the biblical German of Martin Luther. **Blood money** is a translation of *Blutgeld*, and **bloodthirsty** of *blutdurstig(en)*. *Blood*, incidentally, is also a biblical coinage, first appearing in an eleventh-century Anglo-Saxon version of John, "Mine blood is drink" (6:55).

In a more recent turn of events, the *New York Times* reported that Hillary Clinton's campaign for the Senate was accused of accepting **blood money** from a New York Muslim group supposedly linked to Mideast terrorism. (The donation was returned.) As for **bloodthirsty**: the classic has to be Churchill's calling Hitler a "**bloodthirsty** guttersnipe."

BORN AGAIN

reinvented or renewed; of second birth

This term may sound redundant, but it indicates becoming a follower of God through rebirth. It is first expressed in English in John Wycliffe's 1382 literal translation of Jerome's Latin phrase *natus fuerit denuo* ("to be born again"): "When Nicodemus, a ruler of the Jews, questions Jesus about this curious concept, Jesus tells him, 'Verily, verily, I say unto thee, except a man be **born again** [agen], he cannot see the kingdom of God' " (John 3:3). "How can a man be born when he is old?" Nicodemus asks incredulously, adding, "Can he enter the second time into his mother's womb, and be born?" It is then that Jesus makes his point again that the second birth is "of the spirit," insisting, "Ye must be **born again**" (John 3:7).

William Safire, in his *New Political Dictionary* (1993), defined it: "in its new political sense, freshly convinced; or, newly returned to the fold." Charles Colson, the White House counsel convicted in the Watergate scandal, used the phrase ***Born Again*** to title his 1976 bestseller, and Jimmy Carter helped popularize the term ***born-again Christian*** during his 1976 presidential campaign, explaining, "We believe that the first time we're born, as children, it's human life given to us, and when we accept Jesus as our Savior, it's a new life. That's what '**born again**' means."

Safire added, "The phrase is now used in politics with no religious meaning, but with an ironic Carteresque connotation, to mean 'newborn' or suddenly converted." Democrats rejoining the party have been known as "**born-again** Democrats," and liberals against new taxes are called "**born-again** conservatives." Meanwhile, **born again** has become a popular term to describe the recycling of everything from clothes to surfboards, but the prize goes to a recent advertisement that described the new Volkswagen Beetle as the "**born-again** Bug."

BOTCH

(verb) to repair clumsily; to bungle

As familiar to the modern ear (and experience) as this verb sounds, its English origins date back to Wycliffe's Bible where it appears in 2 Chronicles for the first time. The passage explains how workers are restoring the temple "and each feeble thing they **botch** [bocchyn]" (34:10). Although this might come across as a sarcastic swipe at Levite laborers, it is actually a primal usage that denoted "repair" or "patch," the latter being the most likely source for an echoic origin of **botch**. By the early sixteenth century, however, the verb had taken its defining etymological pratfall.

But **botch** also doubles as a noun in Wycliffe and like its twin appears there for the first time. In Isaiah it names the hump on a camel: "bearing upon the shoulders of beasts their riches and upon the **botch** [bocche] of camels their treasures" (30:6). And in Deuteronomy it denotes "plague": "The Lord smite thee with the **botch** [botche] of Egypt" (28:27). Common to each meaning is the Old French word *boce* ("lump," "boil," or "swelling"), and *boce*'s Romantic relatives survive in words like *ball*, *boss* (as in *emboss*), *bossa nova* (the South American dance that literally means "new bump"), and in the popular lawn game *boccie ball* (which is etymologically redundant).

By Coverdale, the verb becomes obsolete, and by the Revised Standard Version, the only remaining Wycliffe coin is the noun phrase "**botch** of Egypt." The verb's alter ego, on the other hand, was able to bungle its way through the centuries. Shakespeare used it half a dozen times, but most directly when he had Henry V dismiss those who "**botch** and bungle up damnation [with pious motives]" (II.ii.115). And Ezra Pound gave it a new rub when he turned it into an adjective—"botched civilization"—in "Hugh Selwyn Mauberley." But current events give it full rein: A Seattle rock group calls itself **Botch** and Blood Brothers. A prominent headline in the January 14, 2001,

Columbus (Ohio) Dispatch warned Ohio State University football fans (eager for a new head coach) that "It's a Long Search but Just Imagine If OSU **Botches** It." And the *New York Times* asked in a December 2000 article: "Are Democrats more likely than Republicans to **botch** their ballots?"

BRAIN

(verb) to hit or strike on the head

Revered as a guide to peace and love, the Bible contains a surprising number of violent actions and words, including the verb "to **brain**." Nowadays that verb tends to suggest a mental picture of the Three Stooges as they take comic turns in striking one another over the head, but its original meaning was far more violent than the Stooges ever acted.

Brain began as an Old English noun. The verb first appears during the fourteenth century in Wycliffe's translation of the Bible, and back then it meant "to kill by dashing the brains out." In Isaiah 66·3, Wycliffe translates God's comments on sacrifice as "That slayeth a beast, as that **brain** [brayne] a dog." (Animal lovers would probably be even more offended by the translation for King James, which is far more graphic: "He that sacrificeth a lamb, as if he cut off a dog's neck.")

Shakespeare tried to use **brain** as a synonym for *think* in his 1611 play *Cymbeline*. There, Posthumus refers to the prophecies of a mysterious "tablet" as "such stuff as madmen / Tongue and brain not" (V.iv.145–46). But that sense never took hold, and today **brain** is still used specifically for a physical attack upon somebody's head. Shakespeare himself probably knew that it was this sense of the verb destined to last. In *Henry IV, Part I*, he used that common meaning in the threat "I could **brain** him with his lady's fan" (II.iii.23).

BROKENHEARTED

(adjective) extremely sad or grief-stricken; full of despair

In the fourth chapter of Tyndale's Luke, Jesus has returned to Nazareth and has gone to the synagogue where, as was his custom on the Sabbath, he quotes from the Book of Isaiah: "the spirit of the Lord upon me . . . to preach the gospel to the poor . . . and to heal the **broken-hearted**" (4:18). The original lines in Isaiah (61:1) and the quoted version in Luke are the only biblical passages in which the compound term appears. By the time of the Revised Standard Version, however, Jesus still quotes Isaiah, but **brokenhearted** has been omitted from that speech—a peculiar move in that the adjective still appears in Isaiah.

A pairing up of the past participles *broken* and *hearted*, **brokenhearted** is one of the infrequent coinages that has grown out of the roots and stems of the English language: *Broken* derives from the Anglo-Saxon verb *breccan* ("to break"), and *hearted* is the past participial form of the Anglo-Saxon noun *heorte*.

Although the biblical sense of "inconsolable despair" has

held its own through the centuries, most everyone today associates **brokenhearted** with the end of a love affair. In fact, anyone growing up with Rick Nelson in the 1950s will automatically be reminded of his 1957 hit "Stood Up" and its catchy refrain, "Stood up, **broken-hearted**, again."

BROTHER'S KEEPER
responsible party; expected caregiver

The first murder in the Bible also results in the first human lie and perhaps the most widely repeated of biblical questions. After Cain is overcome by sibling rivalry and slays his brother Abel, the Lord asks Cain of Abel's whereabouts. "I know not," Cain replies. "Am I my **brother's keeper**?" (Genesis 4:9).

In his 1382 version of Jerome's Bible, Wycliffe translates the Latin *custos fratis* literally as "keeper of my brother." But not until Tyndale's 1530 version of the Pentateuch does the more familiar **brother's keeper** become the preferred term in attempting to evade blame or responsibility. In a recent television movie (*The Man Next Door*), for example, a felon's brother insults an ineffective parole officer with the line "I thought it was your job to be my **brother's keeper**."

Not just male siblings, however, are keepers. A 2001 Hallmark Hall of Fame movie starring Kathy Bates extends the family relationship to *My Sister's Keeper*, and an attorney on the television series *Law and Order* moves beyond familial connection to protest, "I am not my client's keeper."

BUNDLE

(noun) a collection of things fastened together

Not as familiar as "**bundle** of joy" or "**bundle** of nerves," "**bundle** of myrrh" is the expression that started it all. Appearing in Wycliffe's 1388 version of Song of Solomon, the noun occurs in one of several metaphors that describe the poet's love: "My darling is a **bundle** (bundel) of myrrh to me" (1:12). **Bundle** held the metaphor together until the Revised Standard Version, when it was replaced by an unflattering "bag of myrrh." Of the other half-dozen times **bundle** appears in the Bible, Tyndale's phrase "bound in the **bundle** of life" (1 Samuel 25:29) is, perhaps, the most memorable.

Although its origins are obscure, the noun form of **bundle** probably has its roots in the Middle Dutch verb *binden*, which also gives us the verb *to bind*. (The noun *bunch* also has family ties to **bundle**.) As a verb, however, **bundle** is a later, mid-seventeenth-century coinage.

Today both verb and noun seem to share equal time. We "**bundle** up" when it's cold, "save a **bundle**" in tax dollars, design a banking plan that "**bundles** asset management with retail banking" (London *Financial Times*, February 5, 2001), and view a basketball sharpshooter as "a 5-foot-6 **bundle** of 3-point field goals" (*St. Louis Post-Dispatch*, 2001).

BURNT OFFERING

sacrifice by fire; gift offered to God

This phrase, which appears dozens of times in the Bible, first appears in the Geneva Bible (1560) at the conclusion of the story of Noah's ark. Once the flood waters abate, Noah is able to leave the ark and seeks to offer praise to the Lord for sparing him: "Then Noah built an altar to the Lord and took of every clean beast, and of every clean fowl, and offered **burnt offerings** upon the altar" (Genesis 8:20).

It also occurs in a description of one of the most difficult tests of human faithfulness in the Old Testament—the demand of human sacrifice placed by the Lord upon Abraham. The Geneva translators also use it here for the first time: "Take now," the Almighty says in Genesis 22:2, "thine only son Isaac, whom thou lovest, and get thee into the land of Moriah, and offer him there for a **burnt offering** upon one of the mountains which I will show thee of." Abraham, faithfully but painfully, follows the Lord's orders and is given at the last moment a ram to sacrifice in his son's place.

Whether singular or plural, the expression in contemporary usage has been employed for widely varied effect. A July 2000 story in the Cleveland *Plain Dealer*, for instance, described Cleveland Indians pitcher Steve Woodard as "a **burnt offering** placed at the altar of [opposing Boston Red Sox pitcher] Pedro Martinez." The title of a 1975 horror film directed by Dan Curtis and starring Bette Davis is *Burnt Offerings*, and a July 2001 op-ed piece in the *Boston Herald*

("Eco-Clerics Are Biblically Off-Base") asked, "Does God want us to turn off our air conditioners in mid-July and make **burnt offerings** of SUV's?"

BUSYBODY

(noun) one who meddles in other people's affairs

Coined as an alliterative compound of an Old English adjective (*bisig*) and noun (*bodig*), **busybody** meddles its way into English by way of Tyndale's Peter, appearing only two other times in the Bible—both in the New Testament. (Shakespeare, surprisingly, never used it.) Exhorting his audience to share in Christ's suffering, Peter cautiously reminds them "that none of you suffer as a murderer, or as a thief, or as an evildoer, or as a **busybody** in other men's matters" (1 Peter 4:15). The noun kept its New Testament identity until the Revised Standard Version, when it becomes "mischief-maker."

In spite of its biblical dead end, however, **busybody** managed to survive in a 1710 proverb that observes "A **busybody** burns his own fingers" and even to acquire a new meaning late in the nineteenth century: "a mirror attached to a building, reflecting a view of the street." And probably the most useful term for interfering in love came from Edgar Allan Poe, who commented in his "Mystery of Marie Roget" on the practice of "romantic **busybody**ism."

Busily true to its name, **busybody** continues to concern itself with every other part of speech. *Busybodied*, *busybodying*, and *busybodyness* are typical embodiments.

C

CAST THE FIRST STONE

lead the attack; be first to punish

Coined by Tyndale in his version of the Fourth Gospel of the New Testament, **cast the first stone** comes from a shortening of a comment made originally by Jesus. When the scribes and Pharisees take hold of a woman caught in the act of adultery, they place her before Jesus in the temple to test whether he will condemn her for her sin. Jesus is slow to answer them and finally declares: "He that is without sin among you, let him **cast the first stone** at her" (John 8:7). In other words, only a person who has never committed sin has the right to punish the woman. According to John, the accusers all have attacks of conscience and depart ashamed from the temple. Jesus then tells the woman, "Neither do I condemn thee; go, and sin no more." (A century and a half earlier, Wycliffe approximated this popular expression with his translation of the same passage: "first cast a stone into her.")

In *The American Heritage Dictionary of Idioms* (1997), Christine Ammer noted two similar expressions in modern English that turn the tables in an effort to accuse the accusers: "people who live in glass houses shouldn't throw stones" and "the pot calling the kettle black."

On the lighter side, however, a May 14, 2000, headline in *The Nation* used the phrase to question the contemporary political scene: "Who's Left (or Right) To **Cast the First Stone**?" And a sports story from the January 24, 2001, edition of the Glasgow *Herald* told us the name of the person who cast the first stone in a local curling championship. But the title of Chester Himes's 1953 novel *Cast the First Stone* captures the spirit of the original biblical passage. It is the personal retelling of the racism (like the misogyny in the biblical story) that this African American author had to endure as he grew up in the United States during the early twentieth century.

CASTAWAY

(noun) one who is rejected

Thanks to the 2001 blockbuster movie *Cast Away* (and its "cast"), the biblical coinage castaway has recast its hold on the popular imagination. A yoking together of the verb *cast* and the adverb *away*, this versatile noun appears for the first time in Tyndale's 1 Corinthians (and again in 2 Corinthians 13:5). In an extended metaphor, Paul compares the struggle of each member of the new church to the winning runner in a footrace. Self-control, he emphasizes, guarantees the prize: "So fight I, not as one that beateth the air: but I tame my body . . . lest after that I have preached to others, I myself should be a castaway" (1 Corinthians 9:27). Here the noun denotes "loser" or "one who is rejected." The more familiar meaning of "one who is shipwrecked" enters the record in 1799 when William Cowper's poem "The Castaway" was published.

Biblical ties to cast in castaway, however, run deep. For example, Wycliffe coins the noun cast, meaning "something thrown" (Numbers 35:17); Tyndale writes "cast the first stone" for the first time (John 8:7); Coverdale comes up with the phrase "**cast** in thy lot among us" (Proverbs 1:14); and the King James Version gives us "**cast** ashore" (Acts 27:26). But these family connections all originate with the verb form (thirteenth century), which in turn emerged obscurely from the Old Norse verb *kasta*—leaving us with a legacy that spans *forecast* to *overcast*, fishing lines to ballot boxes, horoscopes to movie credits, and shadows to broken bones.

CHILDBEARING

(verbal noun and adjective) the act or process of bringing forth a child; that bears a child

This labor-intensive part of speech—capable of doubling as both noun and adjective—appears in both roles for the first time in Wycliffe's Old Testament. As a noun it refers to Rebekah's giving birth to Jacob and Esau: "The time of **childbearing** [childberyng] came" (Genesis 25:24); and as an adjective it modifies the prophet Isaiah's personification of Zion as a soon-to-be-expecting mother: "I am barren, not **child bearing** [child berende] (Isaiah 49:21).

Compounded of the Old English noun *cild* ("child") and verb *beran* ("to carry or bear"), **childbearing** is virtually translated out of biblical existence after Wycliffe. Hundreds of passages include "child" and/or its many variations, but by King James, **childbearing** is found only in the New Testament: In Paul's First Letter to Timothy, the apostle explains the self-identity of woman. Her transgressions "notwithstanding," he says, "she shall be saved in **childbearing**" (1 Timothy 2:15).

Many of today's women, however, have liberated themselves from doctrinal subordination. According to *The Frailty Myth* (2000), more women have begun to "challenge **childbearing** myths," finding salvation in career opportunities. As "The Hip Mama-Festo" puts it: "the ideal **childbearing** age happens to coincide with the years most important to building a career."

CITY SET ON A HILL

obvious symbol; easily visible example or role model

The Sermon on the Mount is perhaps the most famous of the teachings of Jesus. After listing the Beatitudes ("Blessed are the poor in spirit . . ."), Jesus tells the listening multitudes: "Ye are the light of the world. A **city set on a hill** [set on an hil] may not be hid" (Matthew 5:14). Wycliffe's 1388 translation introduces this now politically nuanced phrase for the first time in the written record of English. The phrase, however, is a rendering of Jerome's Latin, "non potest civitas abscondi supra montem posita," which would be in a rough word-for-word literal translation, "not able to be a citizenry [city] absconded [hidden] on a mount posited [put]." (Wycliffe's 1382 version reads "put on a hill.")

More familiar today as a **city upon a hill**, William Safire's *New Political Dictionary* defined the phrase as "the ideal or shining example; a paragon of civic success or virtue." He pointed to the use of the term in a 1630 sermon, "A Model of Christian Charity." Delivered by John Winthrop aboard the *Arbella*, this sermon attempted to lift up the Massachusetts Bay Colony as the New World's example of civic virtue. "We must consider that we shall be as a **city upon a hill**," Winthrop warned his followers. "The eyes of all people are upon us, so that if we shall deal falsely with our God in this work we have undertaken, and so cause Him to withdraw His present help from us, we shall be made a story and a byword through the world." Historian Lawrence Kennedy, in his *Planning the City upon a Hill: Boston Since 1630* (1992), further immortalized Winthrop's epithet.

But Winthrop's phraseology has long survived in American political rhetoric as well. John F. Kennedy, for example, used the **city upon a hill** reference, and more recently, in his 1989 farewell address, Ronald Reagan also lifted that image, adding a modifier to describe America as the "shining **city upon a hill**."

CIVILITY

(noun) formal politeness that results from respecting social conventions; respectful behavior

The alpha and omega of **civility** is, literally, biblical. The noun occurs for the first time in English in Wycliffe's 1382 Acts of the Apostles, then disappears completely from all subsequent versions of the Bible. (As quickly as Wycliffe's 1388 revision, it becomes "freedom.") The sole passage in Acts involves an exchange of words between Paul and a Roman tribune. Paul asks him if he is a Roman citizen, and the guard replies, "I with much sum got this **civility** [civylite]" (Acts 22:28). By the mid-sixteenth century, this sense of the noun had become obsolete, eclipsed by the familiar connotations of today's usage.

Probably Wycliffe's attempt to translate the Latin *civitatem* from the Vulgate, **civility** was nevertheless current in Old French as a derivation from the Latin *civis* ("townsman") and ultimately from the Indo-European root *kei* ("to lie or dwell at home"). Thus the "how-one-behaves-at-home" connotation takes hold—without preference given to citizen, townsman, or civil servant.

But home is where the heart is, and **civility**, over time, has claimed the hearts of many "homes." Shakespeare, in *As You Like It*, directed Orlando to talk about "smooth **civility**," which ". . . The thorny point / Of bare distress hath ta'en from me . . ." (II.vii.96–97). The seventeenth-century poet Robert Herrick was more "bewitched" by a "wild **civility**" "than when art / Is too precise in every part" ("Delight in Disorder"). Closer to home, a recent headline in the *Pittsburgh Post-Gazette* (February 2001) claimed that George W. Bush moved with "natural **civility**," and Supreme Court Justice Clarence Thomas, speaking at the American Enterprise Institute's Annual Dinner (February 2001), advocated "a strong civil society," not a "timid **civility**."

COAT OF MANY COLORS

multicolored garment; patchwork covering

Not many Bible phrases bring to mind the composer Andrew Lloyd Weber, the country singer Dolly Parton, and former president Bill Clinton.

Coat of many colors, however, is a many-faceted expression that comes from the Old Testament story of Joseph, the youngest of Jacob's numerous sons. It makes its first appearance in written English when the narrator in Tyndale's Genesis (1530) comments that "Israel loved Joseph more than all his children, because he begat him in his old age, and he made him a **coat of many colors**" (Genesis 37:3). The phrase reoccurs two more times in the Chapter 37 story of Joseph's betrayal, but only in the King James Version does it retain the adjective "many." (Tyndale uses "gay," and the Geneva [1560] chooses "particoloured.")

During the late 1960s, Andrew Lloyd Weber wrote a musical stage version of this Bible story and titled it *Joseph and the Amazing Technicolor Dreamcoat*. In 1971, Dolly Parton wrote and recorded "**Coat of Many Colors**," a hit country song about overcoming childhood embarrassment about a patchwork coat her mother sewed. Three decades later, Bill Clinton selected this biblical allusion for his farewell speech. Leaving the presidency in January 2001, Clinton spoke of racial reconciliation: "America cannot lead in the world unless here at home we weave the thread of our **coat of many colors** into the fabric of one America. As we become ever more diverse, we must work harder to unite around our common values and our common humanity."

COMMUNICATION

(noun) the act of transmitting; the giving or exchanging of information

When the American philosopher John Dewey made the point in *Democracy and Education* (1916) that "there is more than a verbal tie between the words common, community, and communication," he was mapping out the territory of a new American pragmatism. Most likely he was unaware that for two of the three words the verbal tie extended to the Bible. Both **common** and **communication** make their English language debut in Wycliffe. (As an historical curiosity, though, **community**, defined as "a state or commonwealth," appears for the first time in Wycliffe's *Selected Works* [III.342].)

Although the first appearance of the most **common** meaning of **common**, "belonging equally to more than one," predates Wycliffe's use of the same adjective by sixty years (his Acts 2:44 was second), **common** does make a first appearance in Wycliffe to denote "generally accessible or familiar"—as in "For to be **common** [comoun] to you" (2 Maccabees 9:27). The word **communication**, on the other hand, is spoken by Paul as he makes his case to the Corinthians for generosity in their gift-giving to the church: "this mystery, which glorifies God in the obedience of your knowledge in the gospel of Christ, and in the simpleness of **communication** [comynycacioun] to him and to all" (2 Corinthians 9:13). Even though Wycliffe translates straight from the Vulgate's "et simplicitate communicationis," **communication** was dropped from this passage in all later versions of the Bible. Starting with Tyndale, "distribution" is preferred, yet by King James, **communication** appears in several other places.

Latin is the etymological tie that binds these three words, but the genealogy is obscure. The simplest reading combines the Latin *com* ("together") and *unus* ("one") so that "a togetherness like oneness" is a literal translation of the compound. However, another way of looking at it takes the Old High German derivation *gimeini* as the true ancestor, a reasoning that accounts for the modern German word for "common" (*gemein*), which undergraduate students of sociology (and Max Weber) learn as the first half of *Gemeinschaft*, usually translated as "community."

The widespread application of **communication** and its siblings today—as both adjective and noun—is **common**place. We travel between the inner space of the **common** cold to a **communications** satellite orbiting the earth—and it all makes perfectly good **common** sense.

CONSCIENCE

(noun) inward knowledge of something, usually the sense of right and wrong

Borrowed directly from the Latin of Jerome's New Testament (*conscientia*), **conscience** scores at least five "firsts" as an

English biblical coinage, appearing only in the New Testament. Three different usages occur in Wycliffe (1 Corinthians 8:7, 2 Corinthians 5:11, 1 Peter 2:19) and two in Tyndale (1 Corinthians 10:25, Romans 14:23). Tyndale also originated the phrase "to have a clear **conscience**" (Acts 24:16).

Although each usage differs in some way, all share the literal meaning of "inward knowledge," which stems from the compounding of the Latin *con* ("with" or "together") and *scientia*, the present participle of the verb *scire* ("to know"). For example, Wycliffe uses the plural for the first time when he addresses the Corinthians: "and I hope that we are open also in your **consciences**" (2 Corinthians 5:11), and Tyndale argues for **"conscience'** sake" for the first time when Paul cautions the same congregation that "Whatsoever is sold in the market, that eat, and ask no questions for **conscience** sake" (1 Corinthians 10:25). All of the Corinthian coinages survive in the Revised Standard Version.

Originally **conscience** was a noun of condition and as such did not have a plural form. In the beginning, so to speak, there was only **conscience**, and still, we continue to say "a" **conscience** or "the" **conscience** rather than **consciences** (in much the same way that we say "common sense" and not "common senses"). Eventually, it became identified with a discreet "thing" possessed by individuals as well as shared by a community or communities. Thus we can hear Jiminy Cricket in Walt Disney's *Pinocchio* (1940) singing to each of us privately, "And always let your **conscience** be your guide," while we read Jonathan Kozol's 1995 book *Amazing Grace: The Lives of Children and the **Conscience** of a Nation.*

CONSUME/CONSUMER

**(verb/noun) to destroy or do away with / one who
consumes**

Both the transitive verb **consume** and its familiar noun form,
consumer, make their first appearances in English via the
Bible. Wycliffe introduces **consume** in Leviticus when the
Lord tells Moses that "All . . . sacrifice of priests with fire shall
be **consumed** [consumyd]" (6:23). And **consumer** turns up a
century and a half later in Coverdale's Book of Malachi, where
the prophet speaks the words of God: "I shall reprove the
consumer for your sakes" (3:11). Here, however, **consumer**
refers to the locust that would devour "the fruits of the soil"
and not to the more contemporary person who uses up articles
of production, a connotation that enters the language about
three hundred years after Coverdale's coinage. No other version, incidentally, follows Coverdale's lead in Malachi. Instead,
the favored word is *devourer*, a loanword from the same passage in Jerome's Latin Bible. By the time of the Revised
Standard Version, many forms of the verb **consume** can be
found throughout the Bible, but **consumer** no longer appears
anywhere in the biblical text.

But this is not the case otherwise. Perhaps because of its
latent connection with buying and selling (the Latin root *sumere*
derives from *emere*, "to buy," which is also the root of *redeem*),
consumer and its first cousin, **consumption**, have become the
watchwords of a global economy. "**Consumer** credit" shapes

the "**consumer** society" of "conspicuous **consumption**" which, in turn, is reflected in the "**consumer** price index."

CONTRADICTION

(noun) a statement in opposition to another statement

Wycliffe borrows **contradiction** straight from Jerome's Vulgate Psalm 54:10 (*contradictionem*) and translates the verse as "I saw wickedness and **contradiction** [contradiccioun] in the city." Subsequent translations not only drop the noun but also edit Psalms 54 and 55 so that this same passage occurs as Psalm 55:9: "for I have seen violence and strife in the city" (King James).

Literally "against speaking," **contradiction** combines the Latin root *contra* ("against") and the verb *diccere* ("to speak"). However, before Wycliffe wrote it into the English language in 1382, the word had existed in Old French (with the same modern spelling) for at least a hundred years.

Given both language cultures, it's not surprising that **contradiction** lends itself in equal measure to the Cartesian tradition of logic (according to the principle of **contradiction**, a thing cannot be and not be at the same time), and to the illogic of contemporary American politics, as headlined in a recent edition of the Minneapolis–St. Paul *Star Tribune*: "Lone Ranger Bush; A Foreign Policy Full of **Contradiction**" (February 2001).

CRIME

(noun) an act committed in violation of a law; something undesirable

When a liberal arts college in Iowa recently offered a new undergraduate elective course called "Crime and Christianity," it was probably unaware of the philological serendipity of the course title. **Crime**, as an English noun, first appears in Wycliffe's New Testament—twice in the Book of Acts.

The first passage occurs in a letter written by the Roman tribune who defends Paul by acknowledging that there was no "**crime** [cryme] worthy the deaths or bonds" (Acts 23:29). The other comes soon after when Festus lays out Paul's case before Agrippa: "It is not custom . . . to damn any man [without having] his accusers present and take place of defending, for to wash away **crimes** [crymes] or great trespasses" (Acts 25:16). Only the latter remains in the Revised Standard Version (one of four passages).

Although **crime** (spelled the same) was current in Old French as early as the twelfth century, Wycliffe apparently borrowed the noun from Jerome's Latin *crimen*, which evolved from the Indo-European root, *krei* (also the source of *scream* and *cry*).

In today's English, "**crime** does not pay" has been, perhaps, the most familiar and unassailable of all the **crime**-ridden clichés. But even that moral maxim now has been called into question by Joel Dyer in his recent book *The Perpetual Prisoner Machine: How America Profits from Crime* (2000).

CUCUMBER

(noun) a creeping annual vine of the gourd family; the fruit of this plant

Wycliffe borrows from the Vulgate Latin *cucumeres* to give us the initial usage of **cucumber** in the English language. The passage occurs in the apocryphal Book of Baruch, where Israel is being told that they will be taken as captives to Babylon and confronted by false gods. Jeremy warns them to remain faithful to the God of Israel, because like a scarecrow in a garden "where **cucumbers** [cucumeris] waxen," these other gods are empty shells (Baruch 6:69). It also appears in the Bible as an adjective: "and the daughter of Zion is left like a booth in a vineyard, like a lodge in a **cucumber** field" (Isaiah 1:8).

To be compared to "a lodge in a **cucumber** field" might not be the most flattering compliment in modern terms, but the "**cucumber**-toning facial sprays" and "**cucumber** skin creams" marketed by today's beauty industry offer an "all natural" means to that metaphorical end. Maybe the Laputan scientist in Swift's *Gulliver's Travels,* "who had been eight years upon a project for extracting sunbeams from **cucumbers**," was onto something after all!

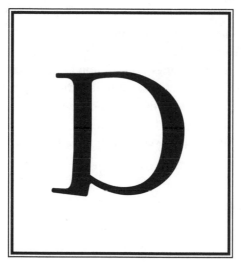

DAYTIME

(noun) the time between dawn and dusk

Originating as two words in Coverdale's Psalm 22:2 ("I cry in the **day time** [daye tyme] . . . and in the night season"), the word as we know it came together seventy-five years later when the King James translators fused the two monosyllables in seven different passages.

Of **daytime**'s siblings, *dayspring* and *daylight* are the eldest (fourteenth century), *daybreak* is slightly younger (sixteenth century), and *daylong* is the youngest (nineteenth century). As for their distant cousin the adjective, it was raised in the twentieth century on the proverbial diet of **daytime** television.

DISHONOR

(verb) to treat with indignity; to disgrace

A good example of meaning in search of a word, **dishonor**, *unnoble*, and *unhonor* were at least three attempts by Wycliffe to English the Vulgate Latin verb *dehonestare* and/or the Old French *deshonorer* (which had been in use since the twelfth century). The honor, however, went to **dishonor**. The passage occurs in the 1388 version of apocryphal Ecclesiasticus: "This seed shall be **dishonored** [disonourid], that passes the commandments of the Lord" (10:23).

Although the more common noun form predates the verb

by nearly a century, and the more familiar adjective *dishonor-able*, shows up about a hundred and fifty years after Wycliffe's coinage, the verb remains in the spotlight of the annual Golden Raspberry Awards, "which **dishonors** cinema's worst offerings."

DOCTRINE

(noun) a rule or principle that forms the basis of a belief or theory; that which is taught as true

Another Wycliffite loanword from the Latin of Jerome's New Testament, **doctrine** enters the written language in the words of Matthew's Jesus, who is quoting Isaiah: " 'This people honors me without cause, teaching the **doctrines** and commandments of men' " (Matthew 15:9). This is the first time that **doctrine** appears in the modern sense of "that which is taught as true concerning a specific area of knowledge" (as in the Monroe Doctrine, when "knowledge" becomes "policy"). Through the seventeenth century it was most commonly understood as "the action of teaching," and Wycliffe claims first rights on this connotation as well: "In all things showing good faith, that they adorn in all things the **doctrine** [doctryn] of our savior God" (Titus 2:10).

The staying power of this authoritative noun might have to do with its learned ancestry. From the Latin verb *docere* ("to teach") and its Greek relatives *dadaskein* ("to teach") and *dokein* ("to seem"), **doctrine**'s siblings include *doctor* (which originally meant "teacher"), *document, dogma, orthodox, doxology*, and *decent*.

And two hundred years after Wycliffe, Shakespeare managed to give it an even wider audience when in *Love's Labor's Lost* Berowne professes that "From women's eyes this **doctrine** I derive; / They are the ground, the books, the academes, / From whence doth spring the true Promethean fire" (IV.iii.298–300).

DOUBTfUL

(adjective) uncertain or unsure about something

We can be reasonably certain that Wycliffe's Book of Ezekiel (1388) is the source of our word **doubtful**, but why the adjective never appears again in subsequent translations of this inaugural passage is puzzling. The context of Ezekiel's oracular warning is the imminent fall of Jerusalem: "For why each vision shall no more be void, neither before telling of thing to coming shall be **doubtful** [douteful] in the midst of the sons of Israel" (Ezekiel 12:24). The next time **doubtful** surfaces is in King James (Luke 12:29 and Romans 14:1), but with the Revised Standard Version, it disappears completely.

That we'll ever know why Wycliffe translates Jerome's Latin *ambigua* as **doubtful** (especially since the Latin cognate is *dubitare*) is **doubtful**. But the Old French verb *douter* had been around since the eleventh century, and both the English noun and verb forms had been current since the thirteenth century.

Today, there is one thing certain about **doubtful**—it will undoubtedly appear in the sports section of the latest newspaper, regardless of the sport: "Moreno **Doubtful** for Friday's [baseball] Game"; "High Tide [a race horse] Is a **Doubtful** Starter"; and "Eddie Pope [with a touch of biblical irony] **Doubtful** with Left Big Toe Sprain" [soccer].

E

EAT, DRINK, AND BE MERRY

party and celebrate with food and drink

"Then I commended mirth, because a man hath no better thing under the sun, than to eat, and to drink, and to be merry; for that shall abide with him of his labour the days of his life, which God giveth him under the sun" (Ecclesiastes 8:15). Like a movable feast of words, this atypically joyful advice from the preacher of Ecclesiastes actually makes its entrée into English as the more familiar **eat, drink, and be merry** with Tyndale's 1526 rendition of Jesus' parable of the rich fool. Making a point about the uselessness of hoarded goods and just deserts, Jesus narrates how a certain rich man decides to store all his "fruits and goods," then tells his "soul" to "take thine ease: **eat, drink, and be merry**" (Luke 12:19).

Restaurants have been quick to adopt this phrase and adapt it for their advertising. The Roadhouse Grill chain has a motto of "Eat, drink, and be yourself!" Planet Hollywood invites diners to "Eat, drink, and feel famous," while the actor Bill Murray operates an eatery for customers to "Eat, drink, and be Murray." Longhorn Steakhouse mixes this cliché (with "Lead, follow, or get out of the way") to produce "Eat, drink, or get out of the way," while a Florida newscast about unsafe restaurant conditions was titled "Eat, Drink, and Be Wary." Perhaps the most outrageous claim comes from Mars 2112 restaurant in New York City: "Eat, drink, and meet Martians."

The Book of Isaiah offers another well-known expression of celebration to those facing destruction: "Let us eat and drink, for tomorrow we shall die" (Isaiah 22:13), an expression later changed by those watching their weight to "tomorrow we diet."

ECSTASY

(noun) a state of rapture, beyond reason and self-control

In his 1382 translation of Acts 3:10, Wycliffe transposes the Vulgate's Latin *extasi* to the quasi–Old French *exstasie*, and for the first time the English language records **ecstasy**. (The modern spelling first appears in 1592 in Christopher Marlowe's play *The Jew of Malta*.) The passage occurs as Peter and John approach the "Beautiful Gate" of the Temple in Jerusalem, where they encounter a lame beggar. When Peter lifts him to his feet, the beggar, miraculously, walks. Those who witness this act of healing, according to Wycliffe/Luke, are "fulfilled with wondryng and **exstasie**." Regardless of how it's spelled, however, **ecstasy** never again appears in the Bible.

Although a direct borrowing from Jerome, **ecstasy** derives from the Greek and means literally "to be placed outside" (of oneself): *ek* ("out") plus *histstanai* ("to put or place"). Today, preferring to say colloquially what the word means etymologically, we describe someone in such a state of being as "out of it." (The hallucinogenic experience induced by one of the current drugs of choice [methylenedioxymethamphetamine] goes by the street name of **Ecstasy**—not exactly what Shakespeare's

Polonius has in mind when he misdiagnoses Hamlet as suffering from "the very **ecstasy** of love" [II.i.99].)

EXCELLENT

(adjective) of the highest quality, exceptionally good

In Chapter 12 of his First Letter to the Corinthians, Paul lists the "spiritual gifts" that the Christian gospel offers, and he saves the "best" of those gifts for last: love. The last sentence of the chapter, "And yet I schewe to you a more **excellent** weye" (1 Corinthians 12:31), is the rhetorical bridge to his so-called "Hymn to Christian Love" (1 Corinthians 13).

Wycliffe's 1382 choice of **excellent** for this passage is a direct borrowing from the Latin Vulgate's *excellentiorum*, the inflected form of the verb *excellere*. The word (and the modern spelling) has been retained in subsequent translations—perhaps because of its etymological correctness: Latin *ex* ("from" or "out of") plus *cellere* ("to rise"), literally "to rise above."

A top-of-the-line Academy Award winner it's not, but the 1989 film *Bill and Ted's Excellent Adventure* captures the comic, bottom-of-the-line banality of contemporary adolescent usage: anything that feels good is "**Excellent!**"—which usually means it's being used every other word.

EXORCIST

(noun) one who drives out evil spirits

Given that the 1973 horror movie *The Exorcist* has had two sequels, the word-as-title of the movie has surpassed the original coinage. **Exorcist** occurs for the first time in the Bible, but only in one place: Wycliffe's 1382 translation of Acts. There, as the narrator unfolds the events, Paul travels throughout Ephesus and acquires a widespread reputation as a miracle worker in the name of Jesus Christ. But when nonbelievers (sons of a Jewish priest) attempt to perform the same acts of healing, they fail miserably: "and some of the Jewish **exorcists** [exorcistis] coming about, attempted to call the name of the Lord Jesus Christ on them that had evil spirits" (Acts 19:13). (The coinage of **exorcist** in this passage was retained by all the major post-Wycliffite translators of the Bible.)

Rooted in the Greek verb *exorkizein*, from *ex* ("out of") and *horkos* ("oath"), *to exorcise* means literally "to 'oath' (or adjure) out of someone [an evil spirit or spirits]." The noun form has survived well into the present, most notably in the Roman Catholic Church, where prior to 1972 (the year before the movie *The Exorcist*, based on a novel by William Peter Blatty, was released), one of the four minor orders of the church hierarchy was the **exorcist** (the other three minor orders were lector, server, and porter). And as recently as September 1, 2000, the *National Catholic Reporter* ran a cover story that set the theme for that entire issue: "The Exorcists."

EYE FOR EYE

reciprocal punishment; justice measured to fit the crime

Punishment should be exactly fitting, according to this standard that first appears in Wycliffe's translation of Exodus 21:24: "**eye for eye**, tooth for tooth, hand for hand, foot for foot." Then in the next book of the Pentateuch, perhaps sensing that they're not seeing eye to eye on what it means to be the Chosen People, the Lord tells Moses, "Breach for breach, **eye for eye**, tooth for tooth: as he hath caused a blemish in a man, so shall it be done to him again" (Leviticus 24:20). The law, however, does not apply exactly the same to loyal servants, as the chapter in Exodus also indicates: "And if a man smite the eye of his servant, or the eye of his maid, that it perish; he shall let him go free for his eye's sake."

The more familiar **an eye for an eye**, however, turns up for the first time 150 years later in Tyndale's New Testament, where Jesus refers to this ancient law, saying, "Ye have heard that it hath been said, **An eye for an eye**, and a tooth for a tooth" (Matthew 5:38), but he immediately counters that ethic, preferring the nonviolent response of "turn the other cheek."

Occasionally the term can be twisted to humorous effect. In the 1992 film *Batman Returns*, Michelle Pfeiffer plays Catwoman, out to get revenge on the man who had taken one of her nine lives. As she prepares to do away with her enemy, Catwoman purrs to him, "A die for a die."

Lest this phrase be dismissed as an ancient form of justice without expression in the modern world, consider this lead of an Associated Press release from Riyadh, Saudi Arabia, in the summer of 2000: "Sobbing and expressing regret for his actions, an Egyptian man had his left eye surgically removed in the first **eye-for-an-eye** punishment in Saudi Arabia in over 40 years, a newspaper reported Monday." The Egyptian was being punished for throwing acid onto another man's face during an argument. The article concludes: "Saudi Arabia's strict interpretation of Islamic law calls for cutting off the hands and feet of thieves. Murderers, rapists, drug traffickers and armed robbers are beheaded."

Mohandas K. Gandhi, the great Indian pacifist of the twentieth century, is often credited with this wiser view of revenge: **"An eye for an eye** leaves the whole world blind."

ꬸEEL

(verb) to search for something, especially by hand; to grope

When in his 1382 translation of Isaiah, Wycliffe chose to translate the Vulgate's *palpare* as "to **feel**," he was tapping into his Old English roots. Although a direct borrowing of the Latin verb might have worked (it gave us *palpable* and *palpitate*), the Old English verb *felan*, with its connotation of "to grope," is the more appropriate choice in this context. (Both the Latin and Old English variants derive from an Indo-European root, *pel*, with connections to *tremble* or *flutter*, hence the connection to *palpitate*.)

The coinage appears when Isaiah forewarns the people of the southern kingdom of Judah that harsh consequences will result if God's way is not followed. He then compares those who do not obey the will of God to the blind who must **feel** or grope for the wall: "as without eyes we . . . **feel** [felid]" (Isaiah 59:10). Later translators of this passage favor the verb *to grope*, making this the first but only time **feel** occurs in this context.

ꬸEMALE

(adjective) belonging to the sex that bears offspring

The English genesis for **female** was Genesis—Wycliffe's 1382 version of it. There, in what has become one of the most familiar passages in the English Bible, we're told that "God made of nought man to the image and his likeness; to the image of God he made him; male [maal] and **female** [femaal] he made them of nought" (Genesis 1:27). Although Jerome renders this adjective as "femina" (woman or the feminine gender), Wycliffe opts for its Latin relative, "femella" (girl or young woman).

Femelle survives in modern French, but the modern English spelling of **female** turns up for the first time in Wycliffe's 1388 version, apparently the result of "male" accommodations. Thus in something like an orthographic parody of the biblical act, **female** is indeed born out of "her" "male" companion. Incidentally, the English adjective *male* predates **female** by seven years, making its first written appearance in Scotland's national epic, *The Bruce*, by John Barbour.

ғ I LT H Y

(adjective) disgustingly dirty or offensive; foul

In the third of Zechariah's eight visions, he sees the high priest Jhesus [Joshua] standing before "the face of the Angel" [of the Lord] "clothed with **filthy** [filthi] clothes" (Zechariah 3:3). This first for Wycliffe does not reflect his usual preference for the Latin of the Vulgate. Instead, he favors the Old English *fylthe* (from *ful*, "rotten" or "lazy") over Jerome's *sordidus* (which, nevertheless, becomes the English coinage *sordid*, by the early seventeenth century).

Filthy, of course, has extended its reach beyond the concrete to the figuratively despicable and depraved. Do the **"filthy** rich" really have **"filthy** minds" and **"filthy** mouths"? In a curious coincidence, the first appearance of **filthy** to describe the morally foul occurs in Coverdale's 1535 version of the Bible—in the other *Z* book of the Old Testament: Zephaniah (3:1).

Another **filthy** first occurs in Tyndale's 1526 translation of the New Testament Book of Titus. There, Paul advises that "a bishop must be faultless . . . no drunkard, no fighter, not given to **filthy** lucre" (Titus 1:11;1:7 in King James). Today the two-word phrase is often used facetiously. **"Filthy** lucre" is the identification for a student-to-student marketplace on the Internet. Also on the World Wide Web is medical advice by Neil Osterweil, with the headline **"Filthy** Lucre: Money Can't Buy You Love, but It Could Make You Sick."

FIRST FRUITS

(noun) earliest products of the soil; first gifts or offering

Another Wycliffe coinage, **first fruits**, is spoken for the first time by Jehovah when he promises Aaron that "Whatever thing they [the people of Israel] shall offer of **first fruits** [fruytis] to the Lord, to thee I have given" (Numbers 18:12). (The annual Jewish observance of Shavuot is still referred to as the Festival of **First Fruits**.)

Primitiae, the Vulgate's Latin equivalent of **first fruits**, occurs earlier in Exodus 23:16, but Wycliffe renders that passage as "chief fruits" (1382) and "first things" (1388). Tyndale, however, chooses the Exodus passage to coin the familiar phrase "the **first fruits** of thy labor." And by the time of the Revised Standard Version, **first fruits** appears in dozens of passages in at least fourteen books of the Bible.

Outside of the Bible, **first fruits** has also continued to fructify, reproducing itself in hundreds of different contexts. We read, for instance, that "Science Gives Blind Dogs Sight: **First Fruit** of Genetic Revolution" (*Ottawa Citizen*, 28 April 2001), and then find out that "the **first fruits** of Tony Blair's mission to unite Europe in an anti-terrorist coalition . . . emerged yesterday" (Glasgow *Herald*, September 20, 2001). Kwanzaa, the African American cultural celebration that begins on December 26 each year, takes its name from a Swahili word for "**first fruits**."

FISHERMAN

(noun) one who catches fish for a living or for sport

Translating the Vulgate's *piscatores* (*piscis* equals "fish"), Wycliffe opts for "fishers" (fischeris), and from Wycliffe's pluralization, Tyndale coins the compound **Fishermen**—the only time the word appears in the Bible. It occurs when Jesus sees two boats on the shore of the Sea of Galilee, but "the **fishermen** were gone out of them, and were washing their nets" (Luke 5:2).

If the English language followed something like a politically correct principle of suffix symmetry ("huntermen and **fishermen**"?), it would have favored Wycliffe's noun, so that today "hunters and fishers" would be the familiar phrase, just as Jesus offers in Matthew 4:19 to make his followers "fishers of men." But in that case, the Gloucester (Massachusetts) High School football team, the **Fishermen**, would probably still be hunting for a mascot.

FULL OF DAYS

aged; having lived many years

In biblical time, old age was known as being **full of days**, and over four hundred years ago Tyndale introduced this phrase to the English language. It occurs in the description of the death of Isaac: "and then he fell sick and died, and was put unto his people, being old and **full of days**" (Genesis 35:29). Similarly, the Book of Job ends with the words "So Job died, being old and **full of days**" (Job 42:17). In the King James Version of an earlier passage, Job, however, expresses a much different sentiment about the fleeting nature of time when he laments, "Man that is born of a woman, is of few days, and full of trouble" (Job 14:1). Whether humans are "of few days" or "full of trouble," God, who is described as being omnipresent, is clearly **full of days**, and is referred to in the Bible as **"The Ancient of Days"** (see entry).

A human life of seventy years, by the way, is full of more than twenty-five thousand days. But the Old Testament figure of Methusaleh is said to have lived to the age of 969 (leading to the expression "as old as Methusaleh"), which would have made his life full of more than three hundred thousand days.

G

GET THEE BEHIND ME, SATAN

deny temptation; turn from disbelief

When Jesus first tells Peter of the coming crucifixion, Peter rebukes his master for making such a dire prediction about himself. Jesus turns away, however, and replies, "**Get thee behind me, Satan**: thou art an offence unto me, because thou understandest not the things that are of God, but the things that are of men" (Matthew 16:23). In the Geneva Bible (1560), the phrasing of this ungodly command occurs for the first time in written English.

"Get behind" can suggest meanings as diverse as "lag or fall behind" and "choose to support," so that a context is needed to make the intention of the phrase clear. A few added words have given the phrase a modern comic twist: "**Get thee behind me, Satan**—and push!"

GLORY

(noun) honor from doing something of great value; worshipful adoration

Wycliffe's Bible came into the English language "trailing clouds of **glory** from God" (apologies to Wordsworth's "Immortality" ode). In each of four different passages, the noun coins new meaning and phraseology. In 1 Corinthians 10:31, for instance, it becomes a moral aim: "Do all things . . .

to **glory** [glorie] of God." In Proverbs, **glory** is that which brings distinction: "The **glory** [glorie] of sons" (17:6). As praise, it occurs in Luke: "**Glory** [glorie] be in the highest things to God" (2:14). And in Romans it denotes the majesty of God: "They changed the **glory** [glorie] of God uncorruptible . . . in to the likeness of an image of corruptible man" (1:23).

One of the more familiar borrowings from the Vulgate (*gloria*), **glory** also enjoyed popular currency in fourteenth-century French as *glorie*, Wycliffe's spelling. (The modern spelling turns up in the sixteenth century.)

True to the word's omnipresence in the Bible, **glory**'s trail is just as unavoidable in the history of the vernacular: from William Driver's 1830 epithet "Old **Glory**," to Julia Ward Howe's "Mine eyes have seen the **glory** of the coming of the Lord," to those nostalgic Herman Hupfeld lyrics that haunt the 1942 movie *Casablanca*: "It's still the same old story, / A fight for love and **glory**" ("As Time Goes By").

ꞬꞦꜱꝒ

(verb) to clutch or take hold of

Verbs that express the sensations of the human body are found throughout the Good Book, and touch is among the most important of those sensations. Related to the Old Norse *grapa* (the source of something like an ancestral declension: "grab," "grip," and "gripe"), the verb **grasp** came into English more than a century before it was also used as a noun. Wycliffe introduces the verb in his 1382 translation of Deuteronomy 28:29: "Thou shalt **grasp** [grassp] in midday, as is wont a blind man to **grasp** in darkness." But by the 1388 version, **grasp** has become "grope," which remains the preference of all subsequent versions of the Bible. In fact, Wycliffe's coinage is the first but only time the word (as either noun or verb) appears in the Bible.

In spite of its biblical demise, however, Wycliffe's word as verb and noun took hold in the language. In 1849, Thomas Macaulay wrote in his *History of England*, "There was little doubt that . . . by **grasp**ing at too much, the government would lose all," and a year later, the American writer Washington Irving picked up the term in *Oliver Goldsmith*, acknowledging "I readily **grasp**ed at his proposal." Almost a century after that, General Omar Bradley warned Americans in a 1948 Armistice Day address that "We have **grasp**ed the mystery of the atom and rejected the 'Sermon on the Mount.' " Although the verb's modern use primarily echoes in a cliché of desperation, "**grasp**ing at straws," these days we try to **grasp** a concept more often than a concrete object.

The noun's literal and metaphoric senses once merged in an 1855 poem by Robert Browning. In what may be his most frequently quoted line, Browning mused in "Andrea del Sarto" that "a man's reach should exceed his **grasp**, / Or what's a heaven for?"

GRAVEN IMAGE

false or artificial divinity

In Wycliffe's 1388 translation of the Second Commandment, he introduces **graven image** to the written record of the English language: "Thou shalt not make to thee a **graven image** [grauuen ymage], neither any likeness of thing which is in heaven above, and which is in earth beneath, neither of those things that are in water under earth" (Exodus 20:4).

Despite the prohibition, however, **graven images** were still produced. In fact, the fall of Babylon is reported by a horseman who announces, "Babylon is fallen, is fallen; and all the **graven images** of her gods [are] broken unto the ground" (Isaiah 21:9). Even later in the Old Testament, a prophet continues to rebuke the unfaithful: "Thy **graven images** also will I cut off, and thy standing images out of the midst of thee; and thou shalt no more worship the work of thine hands" (Micah 5:13).

Presumably these "standing images" are what an *Atlanta Constitution* writer had in mind in his commentary on the 2002 Academy Awards and Oscar parties, where "the towering Oscar statue [serves] as a gilded **graven image**, the Entertainment God we serve" (March 22, 2002).

The phrase can, however, be used both for ironic effect, as in the name of a Glasgow-based design firm called **Graven Images**, and for comic effect: in the Mark Twain novelette *A Murder, a Mystery, and a Marriage* (written in 1876 but first published in 2001 by *The Atlantic Monthly*), a quiet Missouri town is enthralled by a stranger who, according to Twain, "had a high-bred grace of deportment which was the envy and admiration of everybody, and a tongue that could fascinate a **graven image**."

Today's market includes do-it-yourself **graven images**. A boxed kit titled "Create Your Own Goddess" was released by Journey Publishing in 2001. According to the liner notes, the box contains "clay, modeling tool and instructions for creating 15 sacred female figurines."

HANDMAID

(noun) a female attendant or servant

Hand-words, like hand tools, always seem to turn up when you need them. For Wycliffe, it was **handmaid**. Although he had Jerome's "ancillae" at his fingertips (the female noun form of the verb *ancillor*, meaning "to serve"), Wycliffe preferred the short form of the Anglo-Saxon compound *handmaiden*, which had first appeared about eighty years earlier in one of the English translations of the Psalter.

It first appears in the words of the Psalmist: "To thee I lift my eyes; that dwells in heaven. Lo! As the eyes of the servants in the hands of their lords. As the eyes of the **handmaid** [hand-maide] in the hands of her lady" (Psalms 122:2 in Wycliffe's 1382 version but 123:2 in King James). And then in Luke, in what has become known as the "Magnificat," Mary identifies herself as the **handmaid** of the Lord: "for he hath beheld the meekness of his **handmaid**" [hand mayde] (1:48). In the Wycliffite 1388 version of this passage, however, "handmaiden" replaces **handmaid**. Retained in Luke by Tyndale, King James, and the Revised Standard Version, "handmaiden" appears only this one time in the Bible. **Handmaid**, however, can be found in about a dozen passages.

These days **handmaid** is most likely to be associated with Margaret Atwood's 1985 novel *The Handmaid's Tale*, but it also dignifies the name of a Franciscan convent in Harlem: "The **Handmaids** of the most Pure Heart of Mary," one of three predominantly African American orders of nuns in the United States.

HOLIER THAN THOU

appearing more self-righteous than another

Some Bible readers have accused the prophet Isaiah of haughtiness for speaking these words that first appear in English in the 1560 Geneva Bible. Isaiah, however, is merely talking as if he were one of the self-righteous crowd before him, a group that he sarcastically quotes as saying, "Stand apart, come not near to me; for I am **holier than** [then] **thou**" (Isaiah 65:5). The prophet shows his true feelings about such hypocrites when he adds, "These are a smoke in my wrath, a fire that burneth all the day."

From religion, the phrase has spread to politics, music, and psychology: **Holier than Thou** was the name given to the independent Republicans in 1884; it's the name of a record label in the United Kingdom; and a news release from Cornell University criticizes a **"holier than thou** morality study by Cornell psychologists [which] shows why Americans aren't as nice as they think they are."

A popular attack phrase in television drama, the expression was used angrily in one recent episode of the CBS soap opera *The Young and the Restless*: "Mary Williams is a self-righteous old windbag, and I'm sick of her **holier-than-thou** attitude!"

HORROR

(noun) jagged roughness, forbidding ruggedness

The English language first experienced **horror** through Wycliffe's translation of Deuteronomy 32:10—not because of the dreadfulness of his word choice, but because in that passage the noun **horror** enters the written record for the first time. In its prevalent meaning of "dread or terror," **horror** also appears in Wycliffe's Ezekiel 32:10 (same chapter/verse as Deuteronomy!), but a citation in one of the "Legends of the Saints" predates by seven years his use of the noun in this context.

A literal translation from the Vulgate's *in loco horroris* ("in the place of horror"), Wycliffe's noun occurs in the so-called "Song of Moses": "He [the Lord] found him in a desert land, in a place of **horror** [orrour], and of waste wilderness." (Today this *loco horroris* has relocated to the stage and screen as "a little shop.")

The Latin noun derives from its cognate verb *horrere* ("to bristle or shudder") and thus by association describes a rugged or otherwise forbidding terrain. (Undoubtedly the hair-raising scariness of Moses' desert was there too.) Later translators dropped **horror** in favor of more "natural" descriptors, such as "roaring wilderness" (Tyndale) and "waste howling wilderness" (King James). By the Revised Standard Version, only a handful of **horrors** occurs in the Bible.

HOUSE DIVIDED

fragmented home; split interests or lack of unity

After Jesus cures a man possessed by a devil, the Pharisees accuse him of being aided by Satan. The Jesus of the Geneva Bible (1560) responds, "Every kingdom divided against itself, shall be brought to naught: and every city or **House, Divided** against itself, shall not stand" (Matthew 12:25). He expresses a similar sentiment in the next gospel: "Or if a house be divided against itself, that house cannot continue" (Mark 3:25). Forty years earlier, Tyndale's "household divided" was just a syllable away from claiming first usage, and 150 years before that, Wycliffe had the wrong verb, "a house departed."

Abraham Lincoln helped popularize the phrase in his 1858 speech at the Republican State Convention in Illinois: " 'A **house divided** against itself cannot stand.' I believe this government cannot endure permanently half slave and half free. I do not expect the Union to be dissolved—I do not expect the house to fall—but I do expect it will cease to be divided. It will become all one thing, or all the other."

Because of its figurative *and* literal richness, **house divided** has attracted a kingdom of punsters. (That same attraction has claimed over eighty book titles, from mother-daughter incest to the O. J. Simpson trial.) A recent example appeared in the *Washington Post* under the headline "A **House Divided** Comes Together." The story described how the design for the new Anacostia (Va.) Museum and Center for African American History and Culture could have been "a formula for architectural disaster": "one firm did the front of the building and another did the back and they all sort of met in the middle" (March 2, 2002).

HOUSETOP

(noun) the roof of a house or dwelling

As they sit atop the Mount of Olives, Tyndale's Jesus responds to his disciples' questions about when to expect the end of the world and by what signs they will know its approach. Referring to "the coming and close of the age," Jesus forewarns them that in those days the abominations foretold by the prophet Daniel will appear, and when that happens, "let them which be in Judea flee into the mountains: Let him which is on the **House Top** [housse toppe] not come down to take anything out of his house: Neither let him which is in the field return back to take his clothes" (Matthew 24:17–18). This 1526 literal translation of the Greek *doma* ("house" or "housetop") introduces the compound noun into written English for the first time. (Wycliffe chose "house roof.")

By the late nineteenth century, **housetop** had become the figurative place from which to proclaim (or shout) one's devotion to religious and nonreligious ideals. That point of view eventually provided Pat Robertson with the title of his 1972 autobiography, *Shout It from the Housetops*. Today, however, the **housetop** has become virtualized. The London-based **housetop**.com (inspired by the Matthew 24:17 passage) specializes in the production of spiritual video courses for the Catholic faithful. But for many parents and children, up on the **housetop** ("click, click, click") is really the place where "reindeer pause / [and] Out jumps good ol' Santa Claus" (from B. R. Hanby's 1866 song "Up on the **Housetop**").

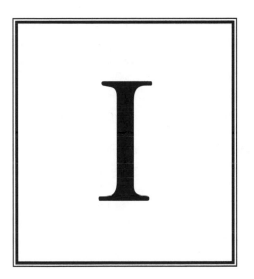

I

INFIDEL

(noun) one who does not believe in the "true" religion

During the three-month period following the September 11 terrorist attacks, the use of **infidel** in the English-speaking news media quadrupled. An informal LEXIS-NEXIS survey of major newspapers revealed that the noun occurred about 60 times between November 10, 2000, and September 10, 2001; however, from September 11 to November 11, **infidel** occurred over 225 times—usually in the context of the Taliban perspective and synonymous with anyone who is non-Islamic.

Infidel is recorded for the first time in the English language also in the context of religious tension and conflict. Tyndale's Paul warns the Corinthian faithful not to be "mismated with unbelievers." Pressing them further, he asks, "What part has he who believes with an **infidel** [infidele]?" (2 Corinthians 6:15).

A faithful borrowing of the Latin *infidelis* (*in* ["not"] plus *fidelis* ["faithful"]), Tyndale's **infidel** actually appears for the first time in the above Corinthians passage and again in 1 Timothy 5:8. As they occur in Tyndale's translation, these were the only **infidels** in the Bible until the Revised Standard Version, when in each verse the **infidels** are translated into "unbelievers."

A second cousin, **infidel**ity (a familiar French term since the twelfth century), made its way into English during the sixteenth century and has enjoyed a unique semantic husbandry (and wifery) ever since.

INTERPRET/INTERPRETATION

(verb/noun) to explain or clarify the meaning of / that which has been so clarified

Over two thousand years before Freud's *The **Interpretation** of Dreams* (1900), Daniel was making a name for himself as someone who could "**interpret** [interprete] dark things and unbind bound things" (Daniel 5:16). In Wycliffe's version of this biblical book of dreams, King Belshazzar asks Daniel "to show to me the **interpretation** [interpretacioun]" (5:14) of the mysterious handwriting on the wall of his palace. Daniel accommodates, but as fate would have it for the king, some things are better left unsaid.

Literally a "go-between" word from the Latin *inter* ("between") and a Sanskrit root, *prath* ("to spread abroad"), both the verb and the noun forms make their English language debut in the Book of Daniel, and both are direct borrowings from the Vulgate. (The Old French verb *interpreter* dates from the twelfth century.)

Today the art of **interpretation** has "unbound" itself from the dream-vision, handwriting-on-the-wall tradition (*pace* Freud), but in so doing has become tangled up in literary theory and postmodernist hermeneutics. (*Hermeneutics* is the Greek word for **interpretation** and comes from Hermes, the messenger of the gods.) From this perspective, every text qualifies for its own version of the multivolume *The Interpreter's Bible*. Over four hundred years ago, Montaigne might have been the first to see the complexity of this handwriting on the wall: "It is more of a job to **interpret** the **interpretations** than to **interpret** the things" ("On Experience," c. 1580).

IRREVOCABLE

(adjective) that which cannot be taken back; irre-versible

Unlike many things in life, translations of the Bible are not **irrevocable**, and the coinage of this otherwise stubborn adjective speaks for itself. It occurs when Wycliffe's Ezekiel vocalizes the word of the Lord: "for I the Lord led out my sword of its sheath **irrevocable**" (Ezekiel 21:5).

Borrowed from Jerome's Latin, *irrevocabilis* (an amalgam of *ir* ["not"] plus *re* ["again"] plus *vocare* ["to call"]), **irrevo-cable** was revoked six years later in the 1388 version by Wycliffe's followers. The Wycliffites preferred instead the literal English translation of the Latin, "[where the sword] may not be called back again." (Wycliffe also introduced the verb *revoke*, but since it appears in a 1380 nonbiblical work, it was not "coined by God.")

Wycliffe's original choice of **irrevocable** is the only time the word ever appears in the Bible.

IVORY TOWER

symbol of unreachable isolation or distorted reality

Since some of the most sensual language in the Bible is found in the Song of Solomon, to find an **ivory tower** in its midst could challenge the understanding of the most pedantic of college professors. Unlike its contemporary denotation of aloof intellectualism, however, Wycliffe's 1382 coinage (and literal translation of the Vulgate's *turris eburnean*) is a simile for the beautiful neck of the poet's beloved: "Thy neck as an **ivory tower** [yuerene tour], thine eyes as the cisterns [cysternis] in Esebon" (Song of Solomon 7:4).

How the beauty of a woman's neck morphed into academic isolationism remains unclear, but beginning in the early twentieth century the allusions to the latter began to steadily increase. In Henry James's unfinished novel *The Ivory Tower* (1917), for example, Graham Fielder asks, "Doesn't living in an **ivory tower** just mean the most distinguished retirement?" Twenty-two years later the British philosopher R. G. Collingwood commented in his *Principles of Art*, "The tendency was for each artist to construct an **ivory tower** of his own: to live, that is to say, in a world of his own devising." (This also applies to those whom the American poet Ezra

Pound referred to as **"ivory tower** aesthetes."*) And that usage has become the common coin for the inhabitants of higher education. In its 2002 publication ranking the best graduate schools, *U.S. News & World Report* highlighted the employment situation by noting that "More newly minted Ph.D.'s are seeking—and landing—great jobs outside the **ivory tower**."

Sometimes, though, the phrase is confused with *ivy tower*, perhaps because of the widespread growth of this plant associated with colleges in the Ivy League. The image of a tower covered with ivy is suggested in "Elegy Written in a Country Churchyard," a 1750 poem in which Thomas Gray writes of "yonder ivy-mantled tow'r."

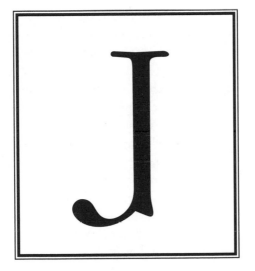

JEHOVAH

(proper noun) the name of God in the Old Testament

In Tyndale's 1530 translation of Exodus, the God of the Old Testament coins his own name, **Jehovah**. It occurs in a conversation with Moses: "I am the Lord, and I appeared unto Abraham, Isaac, and Jacob an almighty God: but in my name **Jehovah** was I not known unto them" (Exodus 6:3).

How this unusual but familiar name came to be has intrigued scholars ever since, and most agree on several key points. It derives ultimately from the ancient Hebrew divine name YHWH, which was considered too sacred to be spoken. To secure that unutterability, readers were directed to "read" the word "Adonai" (a less sacred Hebrew name for God) in place of YHWH. Jerome observes the Adonai tradition for his Latin Bible, as does Wycliffe for his 1382 version. Tyndale, a student of ancient Hebrew, recognizes the significance and propriety of the tetragrammaton (YHWH) in this passage and accordingly "points" those four letters with the Adonai vowels, hence *J*(ah)*H*(oh)*V*(ah). (In the Latin transliteration, the *Υ* became a *J*, and the *W* a *V*.)

Tyndale's "name of names" stuck and appears in all later translations of this passage until the Revised Standard Version, when it is changed to "Lord." Ironically, about the time **Jehovah** was dropped by the Revised Standard translators in 1881, Charles Taze Russell was founding his Watchtower and Bible Tract Society (1884), the organization that would give rise to **Jehovah**'s Witnesses. Today the appearance of **Jehovah** and the currency of its usage are almost exclusively in the context of this worldwide sect and the millions of copies of annual publications associated with it.

JUDGE NOT

apply no value or opinion to others' ideas or behavior

In Tyndale's version of the Sermon on the Mount, Jesus speaks this command for the first time in the written record: "**Judge not** that ye be not judged" (Matthew 7:1). (Earlier, Wycliffe chose to translate Jerome's Latin clause, *Nolite judicare*, as "do not deme.") Jesus also preaches a similar message in the Book of Luke: "**Judge not**, and ye shall not be judged: condemn not, and ye shall not be condemned: forgive, and ye shall be forgiven" (Luke 6:37). And in the Gospel of John, Jesus also advises, "**Judge not** according to the appearance" (John 7:24). A related form of that saying is more familiar today: "You can't judge a book by its cover." Francis Quarles, a seventeenth-century playwright, gave much the same advice about his profession when he said, "**Judge not** the play before the play is done."

On March 4, 1865, Abraham Lincoln drew upon this phrase for his Second Inaugural Address, asking his countrymen not to judge slaveholders: "It may seem strange that any men should dare to ask a just God's assistance in wringing their bread from the sweat of other men's faces, but let us **judge not**, that we be not judged."

A recent article in the *Tampa Tribune* made a slightly different judgment call on this sage advice. Given all the bickering and complaining that often follows in the wake of the decisions that all kinds of judges must make (from bakery contests to the Olympics), they, according to the article, "should be given a break or at least a quick way out of town." The headline read, **"Judge Not**, Unless There's a Getaway Car" (February 14, 2002).

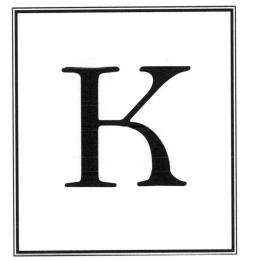

KEYS OF THE KINGDOM

ways to unlock or enter faith

Perhaps the most famous wordplay in the Bible is the pun that Jesus makes in addressing his disciple Peter, whose name comes from the Greek word *petra* ("rock"). Jesus tells him that he will build his church "upon this rock," and in the verse that immediately follows this punning, Jesus promises to give Peter "the **keys of the kingdom** [keies of the kyngdom] of heaven" (Matthew 16:19). Thus Wycliffe keys this literal translation of the Vulgate's *claves regni caelorum* into written English for the first time.

The Keys of the Kingdom was a 1944 religious film produced by Joseph Mankiewicz, but other borrowers of the phrase prefer "keys to" rather than "keys of." In fact, "keys to" various locales have long been celebrated. In *Confessions of an English Opium-Eater* (1822) Thomas De Quincey provided this apostrophe addressed to the drug: "thou hast the keys to Paradise, O just, subtle, and mighty opium!" Mayors still present "the key to the city" as a way to honor visiting dignitaries.

Sometimes the term is shortened, as in the ministries known as Kingdom Keys. Users of this expression, though, are quick to point out that these keys are not necessarily employed easily. Jesus reminds his followers, for instance, that "It is easier for a camel to go through the eye of a needle, than for a rich man to enter into the kingdom of God" (Matthew 19:24).

Modern uses of this phrase tend to emphasize the

entrance to other types of kingdoms, including the Magic Kingdom of Disneyland and Disney World. In 2000, for instance, a nonfiction book by Kim Masters was titled *The Keys to the Kingdom*, with a subtitle referring to the key Disney executive: *How Michael Eisner Lost His Grip*.

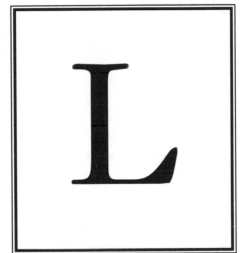

LAND Of NOD

distant biblical area, now a metaphor for sleep

After Cain is cursed for the murder of his brother, Abel, the narrator of the Bible's first book tells us, "And Cain went out from the face of the Lord, and dwelt in the **land of Nod**, on the east of Eden" (Genesis 4:16). Tyndale's 1530 translation of the Pentateuch is the first to introduce this phrase to written English.

Not only did the Genesis verse yield the title of John Steinbeck's 1954 novel *East of Eden*, but it also led to a humorous term for the place we all go to when we fall asleep. Because the verb *nod* has meant to fall asleep, the **land of Nod** became a pun for a place that sleepers visit, as when the satirist Jonathan Swift wrote in *Political Conversations* in the 1730s, "I'm going to the **land of Nod**." The notion of sleep as a form of traveling to another land is an ancient concept, still celebrated in the past century by the lyric of a 1913 song by Stoddard King: "There's a long, long trail a-winding / Into the land of my dreams."

"Sometimes even Homer nods," the Roman poet Horace observed, although Alexander Pope came to the defense of the Greek poet in his 1711 *An Essay on Criticism*: "Those oft are stratagems which errors seem, / Nor is it Homer nods, but we that dream."

The **land of Nod** is not always considered pleasant, because the idea of punishment continues to haunt the figure of Cain. When the French explorer Jacques Cartier first reached the desolate Canadian shore of the Gulf of St. Lawrence in 1534, he commented, "I think it likely that this is the land God gave Cain." Today, however, the **land of Nod** is almost synonymous with the "land of God" in that it is used positively to promote everything from cinnamon buns to bed-and-breakfasts.

LEFT WING

(noun) the left side of an armed force in battle array; the more liberal section of a political party

An unimposing hybrid of power and politics, warfare and ideology, **left wing** takes center stage for the first time in Coverdale's 1535 account of the last book of the Apocrypha, Maccabees. As Judas Maccabaeus, the heroic defender of Judaism and religious freedom, battles his way to victory against all odds, we're told that "when they which were of the **left wing** [lefte wynge] saw that the right side was discomfited they followed Judas behind" (1 Maccabees 9:16).

Some 250 years later the French National Assembly made popular the political seating arrangement that places the radicals on the left side of the presiding officers, the moderates in front, and the conservatives on the right side. Most likely these conceptual combatants then took sides on the political battlefield, thus switching "sides" for "wings."

By the late nineteenth century, socialists were being referred to as "the radical **left wing**," while on the soccer and hockey battlefields, the **left wing** had been reduced to a single combatant positioned to the left of his teammate playing center.

LEGACY

(noun) anything handed down by a predecessor; bequest

One of Wycliffe's major linguistic **legacies** is the infiltration of the English language with many loanwords from the Vulgate Latin of Jerome's Bible. His literal borrowing of **legacy**, however, led to a semantic as well as a translational dead end.

The noun appears in a section of 2 Corinthians where Paul exhorts the faithful to become "ambassadors of Christ": "Therefore we are set in **legacy** [legacie] . . . for Christ" (2 Corinthians 5:20). "Ambassador" would be the English translation of Jerome's word *legationem* (from the verb *legare*, "to send an ambassador"), but Wycliffe chose to stay with the Latin. Consequently, **legacy** was dropped from the 1388 Wycliffite version, never to appear again anywhere in the Bible, and its literal meaning of "legateship" became obsolete by the end of the eighteenth century.

Today, traces of that earlier coinage survive in *delegate*, but the most common **legacy** has been in the sense of a figurative bequest. Thus the first annual Hurston/Wright **Legacy** Award was recently announced to honor published writers of African descent. (The name of the award commemorates the literary contributions of Zora Neale Hurston and Richard Wright.) But perhaps Shakespeare said it best in *All's Well That Ends Well*: "No **legacy** is so rich as honesty" (III.v.13).

LIBERTY

(noun) freedom or release from bondage

John Stuart Mill wrote an entire treatise on it; a Jeep sport-utility vehicle, a college football bowl game, and a statue have been named for it; nations have been conceived in it; and people would choose to die rather than to be without it. As for Wycliffe's Paul, where the spirit of God is, "there is **liberty** [liberte]" (2 Corinthians 3:17).

Although this carryover coinage from the Vulgate's *libertas* (from *liber*, "to be free from") had been current in French since the early fourteenth century, Wycliffe's use of it in this New Testament passage is the first time **liberty** appears in written English. (Four years later in *The Canterbury Tales*, Chaucer uses it for the first time in a secular context.)

Surely another *On Liberty* would be needed to praise the utility of this free-spirited noun. Its liberal use is evident throughout the Bible, Shakespeare, and every other testament to the human spirit that can be translated into language. The nineteenth-century English essayist William Hazlitt seemed to capture the restlessness of this human/divine balance when he avowed that "The soul of a journey is **liberty**, perfect **liberty**,

101

to think, feel, do just as one pleases" (*Table Talk*, 1821–22). Were Hazlitt alive today, however, **Liberty** Mutual Insurance Company would undoubtedly appraise that philosophy of "life, **liberty**, and the pursuit of happiness" as too much of a risk for one of their insurance policies.

LIQUID

(adjective) said of a substance that readily flows; fluid

The first time that **liquid** appears in the written record of the English language is in Wycliffe's Ezekiel, where the prophet includes in his list of temple ordinances "all **liquid** [liquyd] sacrifices" (Ezekiel 44:30). However, Wycliffe's choice of **liquid** for this passage does not stand on solid ground. In fact, this particular "first" might be a slipup.

The adjective derives from the Latin verb *liquere* (the same root as for "liquor"), and it would have been a routine move for Wycliffe simply to use the Latin equivalent in his English translation. But in the Vulgate passage there is no Latin equivalent of **liquid**; instead, "libation" (*libamentum*) appears. (Oddly enough, elsewhere in Ezekiel 20:28, Wycliffe does use "libation" for the first time in English.) Apparently conscious of the misreading for the 1388 version, Wycliffe's followers changed **liquid** to "moist," and **liquid** never again appears in the Bible.

Nevertheless, **liquid** has since morphed into every other

part of speech and has therefore become a valuable asset to the English language. Today we "liquidate" and "liquefy," puzzle over "liquidities" and "liquid gas," and muse with Shakespeare as a "strong-ribbed bark through **liquid** mountains cut" (*Troilus and Cressida*, I.iii.40).

M

MINISTRY

(noun) the rendering of a service, especially as it pertains to religion

Both the secular and religious meanings of **ministry** are introduced in Wycliffe's 1382 translation of the Bible: Ezekiel promises to make the faithful "porters of the house, in all the **ministry** [mynysterie] thereof" (Ezekiel 44:14), and Paul directs the Colossians to "see the **ministry** [mynisterie] that thou hast taken of the Lord that thou fulfill it" (Colossians 4:17).

In both cases Wycliffe borrows the Vulgate's use of the Latin word for "office" (*ministerium*), but the latter usage has accrued enough meaning over the years so that today the noun is unmistakably (although not solely) associated with the Christian Church. Nonetheless the European practice of naming government departments **ministries** and the directors of those departments *ministers* certainly has been the norm. (American usage seems to have favored *administer* as the verb in this context.)

In an altogether different context, when Coleridge (a minister of language and poetry in his own right) taps **ministry** for his poem "Frost at Midnight" (1798), he could have easily been wondering about the fatefulness of words as they appear and disappear in the never-ending ministrations of language: "Or if the secret **ministry** of frost / Shall hang them up in silent icicles, / Quietly shining to the quiet moon."

MUTTER

(verb) to speak in low, barely audible tones

Because the Vulgate uses the verb *mussitare* in this key passage from 2 Samuel, Wycliffe carries that word over as "musing" [musynge] in his 1382 version of the Bible. The 1388 Wycliffite followers, however, had second thoughts about that choice and apparently decided that the Middle English cognate of **mutter**, *moteren*, was the more appropriate verb. In addition to its Latin, Middle English, and Germanic relatives, **mutter**'s ancestry goes back to the Indo-European root *mu* ("to close"), which has mutated into other "closed off" English words like *mope* and *mute*. (See **mystery**.)

You can almost hear Wycliffe's followers **muttering** to themselves about what word to use in their 1388 translation as David overhears his "servants speaking privately . . . **muttering** [moterynge]" (2 Samuel 12:19). Subsequent translators preferred "whisper," so that **mutter** never appeared again in this passage. (Later it turns up two other times in Isaiah.)

By the nineteenth century, Robert Browning had added a reverse spin to this biblical coinage. In his 1845 poem "The Bishop Orders His Tomb at Saint Praxed's Church," the bishop imagines his mortality: "And then how I shall lie through centuries, / And hear the blessed **mutter** of the mass, / And see God made and eaten all day long. . . ."

MY CUP RUNNETH OVER

complete satisfaction; overflowing pleasure

According to *USA Today*, a recent survey revealed that the favorite book of Bible readers is the collection of Psalms, the most famous of which is easily the Twenty-third Psalm, where David recounts the many divine blessings given to him: "Thou doest prepare a table before me in the sight of mine adversaries; thou doest anoint my head with oil, and **my cup runneth over**" (Psalms 23:5). The Geneva Bible translators were the first to English this memorable line. (Wycliffe's Psalm 22 at that time literalizes the Latin of Jerome's Vulgate Bible: *calix meus inebrians* ("my cup saturating itself" or, for the nonpuritanical, "my inebriating cup"). Wycliffe renders it "my chalice makened full drunk" (1382) and "my cup filling greatly."

Nowadays the expression is mainly used either in pleasure or in mock surprise at any overabundance. For instance, *The Fantasticks*, the 1960s Off-Broadway musical that closed in 2002 after the longest run of any show in American theater history, features a plaintive ballad with the lyric that "**my cup runneth over** with love." On the Internet, the phrase labels everything from espresso sales to sprinkler games. A Web request for doll supplies apparently left one advertiser overwhelmed by the response: "Post a follow-up," she writes. "**My cup runneth over**."

MYSTERY

(noun) something unexplained or kept secret

Wycliffe is the first to use **mystery** in its familiar religious sense of "a truth known from divine revelation," and except for an earlier passage in a twelfth-century fragment, he is also responsible for giving it currency in its first nontheological meaning. The former occurs in Paul's Letter to the Romans: "The revelation of **mystery** [mysterie] held still . . . in times everlasting . . . which **mystery** is now made open by scriptures of prophets" (Romans 16:25). The latter is found in Daniel: "The **mystery** [mysterie] which the king asks, the wise men . . . must not show to the king" (Daniel 2:27).

Another loanword from the Latin of Jerome's Bible (*mysterium*), **mystery**'s history dates back to the Indo-European root *mu*, signifying "to close" (see **mutter**), an association that led to the *mysterion* (the secret cultic rituals) of the pre-Christian Greek and Middle Eastern religions. (Initiates of these rites were called "mystes," more broadly referred to as "mystics" today.) These "pagan" rituals were then customized by the early Christians so as to accord with a reconceptualization of revealed truth as the divine revelation of the New Testament, thus Paul's claim that "the **mystery** is now made open."

But even as a biblical coinage, **mystery** evokes **mystery**. Wycliffe's single use of the noun to denote a nonreligious phenomenon disappears after the 1382 translation—not only from Daniel but from the Old Testament entirely. The Old

Testament, in other words, is without **mystery**. (When the sense requires it, "secret" is usually the noun of choice.) The New Testament, however, is wrapped in **mystery**. There the noun occurs nearly thirty times, and twenty of those appear in Paul's writings.

NEEDLEWORK

(noun) sewing or design work done with a needle

Needlework is an Old Testament word, appearing almost exclusively in Exodus, where it occurs about eight times and for the first time in written English. In Wycliffe's 1382 version of Exodus 26, the Lord, speaking to Moses, has extended his "bricks and mortar" blueprint for the building of the tabernacle to include all of the ornamental detail work: "Ten curtains . . . diversified with **needlework** [nedle werk], thou shalt make" (Exodus 26:1).

As was the case for many of Wycliffe's coinages, after the 1382 translation, **needlework** was dropped from all later versions of this passage (but retained elsewhere). Except for the King James translators ("cunning work"), most preferred the French derivative *broidery*, another Exodus coinage for which Wycliffe also is credited. (The more familiar *embroidery* turns up in English ten years later in a nonbiblical text, and *needlepoint*, the closest living relative, enters the written record in the mid-nineteenth century.)

Even though the connotative range of **needlework** is sewn up in its skill-specific denotation, a film reviewer for the *Atlanta Constitution* managed to keep some of the readership in stitches with a wry one-liner about the 1995 movie *How to Make an American Quilt*: "The **needlework** is the sharpest thing here."

NETWORK

(noun) any arrangement of wires, threads, etc. that crisscross one another at regular intervals; mesh

For the past 450 years, this coinage of the 1560 Geneva Bible has cast a wide net of meaning over the semantic field of the English language—from broadcasting and computers to police and terrorists (including the title of a 1976 movie starring Faye Dunaway and William Holden). Even as this entry is being written (December 2001), an advertisement has come in the mail for a new book entitled *The Moment of Complexity: Emerging Network Culture.*

One of the main reasons for the increase in **network**'s connections is that during the late nineteenth century it underwent a functional shift from noun to verb (in the context of railroads networking with other regions of the country). But this weblike noun first enters the written record in the Book of Exodus, where it describes that part of the altar in the tabernacle upon which sacrifices are to be made. The Lord instructs Moses as to the fine points: "Thou shalt make unto it a grate-like **network** [networke] of brass" (Exodus 27:4). Prior to Geneva it was simply "net," and since 1560 **network** has been retained in this passage as well as in five other (Old Testament only) passages throughout the Bible.

In one of those intriguingly weird word coincidences, two words starting with *n* connected themselves to the noun *work* and appeared for the first time in English in the same text (Exodus), separated in time by almost two hundred years (from Wycliffe to Geneva) and in space by only one biblical verse (from 26:1 to 27:4): **needlework** (see entry) and **network**.

NO MAN CAN SERVE TWO MASTERS

divided loyalty is impossible

William Tyndale was the first to use this clause in written English. It occurs in his 1526 translation of the Sermon on the Mount, where Jesus decries: **"No man can serve two masters**. For either he shall hate the one, and love the other: or else he shall lean to the one, and despise the other: ye cannot serve God and mammon" (Matthew 6:24). Very similar words are also spoken by Jesus in Luke 16:13. (Wycliffe rendered the same passage as "no man may serve two lords.")

From "no man," the phrase has become gender-neutral as "no servant" or "no one can serve two masters." Another modern variation exclaims, "You cannot be the slave of two masters!" And a current collection of "Words of Wisdom" on the Internet includes these observations: "No fish is caught twice with the same bait. No gains without pains. **No man can serve two masters**."

Usually the expression indicates the impossibility of maintaining divided loyalty, but sometimes that attempt can also backfire. In a *USA Today* review of *Welcome to New York*, a TV sitcom starring Jim Gaffigan and Christine Baranski, Robert Bianco wrote: "Predictably, the not entirely welcome result is what you get when you try to serve two masters and serve neither well. Gaffigan seems oddly shunted aside; Baranski seems shoved in and intrusive" (October 11, 2000).

NOT LIVE BY BREAD ALONE

needing more than food or physical nourishment

Some Bible phrases are so "full of days" that they appear in both the Old and the New Testaments. Moses speaks to his people in the King James Version Old Testament of God's generosity, noting "that man doth not live by bread only, but by every word that proceedeth out of the mouth of the Lord doth man live" (Deuteronomy 8:3). But it's not until the same translation's New Testament that the more familiar "bread alone" appears for the first time. (All prior translations favor "only.") There, Satan's temptation of Jesus includes an effort to make him break a forty day fast in the wilderness by turning stones into bread. Jesus answers with these words: "It is written, 'Man shall **not live by bread alone**,' but by every word that proceedeth out of the mouth of God" (Matthew 4:4).

Bread is meant to represent food or any physical nourishment in this saying, as it does in the use of "break bread" for "eat." In the nineteenth century, the American essayist Ralph Waldo Emerson extended the thought by explaining, "Man does **not live by bread alone**, but by faith, by admiration, by sympathy."

The phrase is tinged with irony today. The Bread Alone

Project describes itself as "Seattle-based rock bands aiding the homeless by fund-raising projects that are recorded," and the company Bread Alone markets itself as "a family of European-style bakeries with locations throughout the United States and headquarters nestled in the Catskill Mountains." Variants have often substituted another product for the bread. On a classic 1970s television commercial for Skippy Peanut Butter, two grocery clerks were seen in a store filled with jars of Skippy; when one clerk pointed out, "Man does not live by peanut butter alone," the other agreed: "Well, we'll sell bread too."

NOVELTY

(noun) something new or unusual

When in 1817 Coleridge proposed that the imagination "reveals itself in the balance or reconciliation of . . . the sense of **novelty** and freshness, with old and familiar objects," he was probably not talking about the "cursed **novelties** [noueltees] of voices" (1 Timothy 6:20) that Wycliffe's Paul has in mind when he warns of the dangers posed by the then new Gnostic beliefs.

Another loanword from Jerome's Vulgate, this "new" Anglicized noun comes from the Latin word for "new" (*novus*), which also gives us the seventeenth-century English coinage for a prose narrative, *novel*. Wycliffe's version, however, is the first and only time **novelty** appears in the Bible. Ironically, the later (imaginative) translations of this passage support

Coleridge's claims for the imagination as a mental balancing act: "unghostly vanities of voices" (Tyndale), "profane and vain babblings" (Geneva and King James), and "godless chatter" (Revised Standard Version).

Although in contemporary society **novelty** shops are becoming old news, and the cash register key labeled **novelties** has become nearly obsolete, **Novelty**, Ohio (near the tiny community of Newbury, Ohio), still challenges the imagination because it exists in name only as a postmark of the U.S. Postal Service.

NURSE

(verb) to breastfeed or otherwise care for an infant

As a biblical coinage, **nurse** hits the jackpot. It goes on record as a verb in Tyndale's 1530 version of Exodus when Pharaoh's daughter commands a Hebrew woman (Moses' mother) to "take this child [Moses] away and **nurse** it for me" (Exodus 2:9). As a noun it surfaces in the Wycliffite Genesis of 1420, about thirty years after an earlier reference in a nonbiblical work. (The dates are questionable.) And as a participial adjective, **nursing** appears for the first time in print in Coverdale's Isaiah as the prophet assures his people in exile that "kings shall be thy **nursing** [noursinge] fathers, and queens shall be thy **nursing** mothers" (Isaiah 49:23).

That the early English spellings of **nurse** resemble "nourish" is no coincidence. In Wycliffe's 1382 version of Exodus

117

2:9, for example, the word is "norisch," a literal translation of Jerome's Latin verb, *nutrire* ("to nourish"), the same root that gives us *nurture*, *nutrition*, and *nutrient*. *Nourish* predates **nurse** in English by about a century and made several of its own first appearances in the English Bible.

By the time Shakespeare wrote *As You Like It* (1600), **nurse** was promoting the growth of other English coinages. In Jaques's famous "All the World's a Stage" monologue, we learn that in this life men and women play many parts, and Act One is the infant "Mewling and puking in the **Nurse**'s arms" (II.vii.144). By the way, this was the debut performance in English for the verb "to puke."

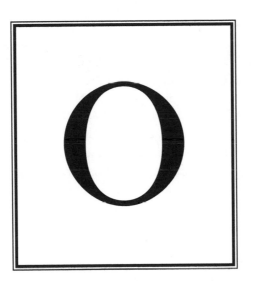

OFFEND

(verb) to make a mistake morally; to transgress

A utility-player word that got its start from the linguistic generosity of a Latin root, **offend**'s siblings include a fraternal twin (*offense*), another set of twins (*defend/defense*), and distant aphetic cousins (*fend* and *fence*). Like de*fend*, **offend** combines a prefix, *ob* ("against"), and the root *fendere* ("to hit or strike"). As an intransitive verb that connotes moral failure ("to have a strike against you"), it debuts in English when Wycliffe borrows Jerome's use of the Latin word *offendere* ("to hit or strike against"): "we **offend** [offenden] in many things. If any man **offends** [offendith] not in word, this is a perfect man" (James 3:2). Although Chaucer was probably the first (only by a few years) to use the more familiar transitive verb form ("It **offends** me") in "A Complaint to His Lady," it was later the King James translators who gave us the "authorized" version of that usage: "if thy right eye **offends** thee, pluck it out" (Matthew 5:29).

In addition to the abstract meaning of **offend**, the verb in its literal or concrete sense of "to bump against something" or "to trip so as to stumble" enters the written record via Wycliffe and Zechariah. As the prophet claims ultimate victory for the people of Israel, he promises that even those who stumble and are weak, "he that shall **offend** [offende] of them in that day" (Zechariah 12:8) shall be given strength. But perhaps a clearer example of this literal meaning is conveyed by one of Wycliffe's biblical coinages of the noun **offense**: "Not before the blind thou shall put [a] thing of **offense** [offence]" (Philippians 1:10). Today this dated usage has mutated into the jargon of contact sports, where an **offensive** (or defensive) lineman must be "blocked" or otherwise "fended" off.

This is not to dismiss the figurative evolution of **offend**. In fact, nowadays we are **offended** by or take **offense** to just about everything and, consequently, are always in need of a lawyer to *de*fend us. Maybe it was Henry James who first crossed the line: "The real **offense,** as she ultimately perceived, was her having a mind of her own at all" (from the 1881 novel *The Portrait of a Lady*).

P

PASSOVER

(noun) the name of a Jewish holy day commemorating the Hebrews' liberation from Egyptian slavery

Tyndale's translation of Exodus (1530) includes **Passover** for the first time in written English, probably his own translation of the Hebrew word *pesach*, which literally means "a passage." (Jerome opted for the Latin noun *transitio* and Wycliffe for "passing forth.") In context the Lord is giving instructions to Moses and Aaron on how the enslaved Israelites should prepare the sacrificial lamb for the night that He will pass through the land of Egypt and "smite" all of the first born: "And you shall eat it in haste, for it is the Lord's **Passover** [passeouer]" (Exodus 12:11).

The feast day of **Passover**, which occurs annually in March/April, celebrates this "passing over" of those who had been instructed to mark their doors with the blood of the lamb, thus protecting their firstborn from "the vengeance of the Lord." The celebration in most traditions lasts for eight days.

Over the years, the verb *to pass* has attracted other prepositions, and most of these combinations have been recent coinages: We can be "passed over" for a raise or promotion, "pass out" at the sight of something horrific (or from too much intoxication), "pass through" a town, "pass up" an invitation to an event, and without the right "password," try to "pass ourselves off" as someone we're not.

PEACE OFFERING

(noun) a gift offered to end conflict or obtain peace

Coverdale's 1535 version of the apocryphal Book of Maccabees gives us this all-too-familiar term but none-too-common practice. Most likely his choice of words was influenced by the Vulgate's use of *pacificorum* ("peace gift"). From the text we learn that the tyrant Antiochus has forbidden the Israelites to practice their religion or to otherwise be free. This includes "burnt offering, meat offering or **peace offering** [peaceoffringe]" (1 Maccabees 1:45).

Whether it's prompted by a domestic squabble, an international flashpoint, or a corporate attempt to buy off legal problems (recent headline: "Napster's $1 BN **Peace Offering** Spurned"), this modern-sounding offspring of biblical translation continues to be the standard-bearer for human decency and well-being. But just to make sure we don't forget that ideal, there's inevitably a "peace officer" nearby who will help us remember (without, we hope, the need to draw his trusty "piece," or "peacemaker").

PERSUASION

(noun) the act of convincing someone to do or believe something

Whatever Tommy James & the Shondells had in mind when they released their 1969 hit single "Crystal Blue **Persuasion**," or what Jane Austen was brooding over when she published her novel *Persuasion*, chances are it wasn't the Bible. But it is in Wycliffe's version of Paul's Letter to the Galatians that the noun is first recorded in English. There, Paul argues *against* a revival of the Mosaic law and *for* the Christian doctrine of justification by faith alone. He wonders who or what has been influencing the Galatian congregation and tells them that "this **persuasion** [persuacioun], or soft moving, is not of him who called you" (Galatians 5:8).

From the Latin verb *persuadere* (*per* ["thoroughly"] plus *suadere* ["advise or urge"]), which is also the root of *suave, assuage, sweet,* and *Suada* (the Roman goddess of **persuasion**), this sweet-talking noun appears in the Bible only in this one citation.

PILLAR Of SALT

a person made inanimate

When the Old Testament God decides to destroy the cities of **Sodom and Gomorrah** (see entry), He warns Lot to flee with his family and not look back lest they be destroyed. Lot and his daughters escape, the narrator of the first Bible book says, adding, "and Lot's wife looked behind her, and was turned in to a **pillar of salt**" (Genesis 19:26). This is how William Tyndale introduces the phrase to the written record of the English language. In the first English version of the Bible, however, Wycliffe translates Jerome's Latin phrase, *statuam* *salis* (literally "statue of salt"), as "image of salt."

The transformation of Lot's wife into something inanimate underscores the importance of salt to human sustenance (see **salt of the earth**). "Ye are the salt of the earth," Jesus tells his followers, "but if the salt have lost his savour, wherewith shall it be salted?" (Matthew 5:13). In the example of Lot's wife, however, she is unable to turn her back completely on the sinful city and is consumed.

Shirley Jackson, author of "The Lottery," also published a 1949 short story titled **"Pillar of Salt,"** which chronicles the mental disintegration of a woman overwhelmed by her phobias in New York City. In her efforts to flee from that modern Sodom, however, the hapless woman becomes paralyzed with fear, almost the living equivalent of a **pillar of salt** (unlike the inanimate object that Lot's wife became).

More recent uses of the phrase include the name of a Christian rock band in New York. And, alternatively, another contemporary rock band, Monster Magnets, uses the phrase in the lyrics of their song "Heads Explode," where the lead singer declares, "I am a **pillar of salt**, you'll never be worse than me."

PLAGUE

(noun) anything that can be a deadly affliction; scourge, epidemic

Plague shares an Indo-European ancestry with *flaw*, *flog*, and *flagellate*, and as a biblical coinage comes directly from the

Latin of Jerome's Bible, the noun *plaga* ("a blow or wound; misfortune").

The key word in a curse that Shakespeare used often (and memorably in *Romeo and Juliet*'s "A **plague** o' both your houses!"), **plague** is found hundreds of times throughout the Bible, where it appears for the first time in written English in Wycliffe's 1382 version of the Book of Revelation. There John's apocalyptic vision expands to include the attack of the horse-demons exhaling fire, smoke, and sulphur, and "of these three **plagues** [plagis] the third part of man is slain, of fire, and of smoke, and of brimstone" (Revelation 9:18). The *Left Behind* novels by Tim LaHaye and Jerry B. Jenkins are based on John's visions.

The word, like its reality, has a long, communicable history. A recent survey of current book and film titles turned up more than three hundred works that use the noun either within the title or as the title itself. Some are canonical: Daniel Defoe's 1722 work of historical fiction, *A Journal of the Plague Year* (based on the 1664–65 Great **Plague** of London) and *The Plague*, the English translation of Albert Camus's 1947 novel *La Peste*. (Not so successful was its 1992 film adaptation, starring William Hurt.) Others seem to be seriously afflicted, like the 1966 horror movie *The Plague of the Zombies*. In today's HIV and bioterrorist culture, however, it's not surprising to find on the bookshelf a progression of titles that suggest John's revelation is at hand: *The Coming Plague* (1995), *Plague Time* (2000), and *After the Plague* (2001).

PROBLEM

(noun) a question or puzzle posed for solution

Today there are no **problems** in the Bible. Even though the word was in the beginning, at least for this word, the Bible was a dead end.

Its English **alpha and omega** (see entry) occurs in Wycliffe's Book of Judges and the story of Samson. At their marriage feast, Samson and his unnamed Philistine wife are entertaining guests when he decides to pose a riddle as a wager. When the guests realize they cannot offer a solution, they threaten to kill Samson's bride if she does not convince him to "show . . . what betokens the **problem** [probleme]" (Judges 14:15). Wycliffe's decision to use Jerome's Latin *problema*, however, was never endorsed by any subsequent translator. It was Tyndale, nearly 150 years after Wycliffe, who solved the **problem** for all future translators by rendering the noun as "riddle."

But Wycliffe's original choice is not so problematic if considered from the etymology of **problem**. Transliterated into Latin from Greek, the noun adds the prefix *pro* ("forward") to the root verb form *ballein* ("to throw"), from which survives the colloquial expression, "Let me throw this out to you," i.e, "Let me pose this question."

The Bible notwithstanding, **problems** have been and continue to be a fact of life. As early as 1609, the adjective *problematic* found its way into the language, and by 1630, Ben Jonson was satirically "problematizing" (his coinage) the human condition. Two hundred and seventy years later, in an address delivered to the Pan-African Conference, W. E. B. Du Bois identified "the **problem** of the twentieth century [as] the **problem** of the color line," a claim echoed a generation later by Eldridge Cleaver when he announced that "you're either part of the solution or part of the **problem**." A few years earlier, Betty Friedan was speaking out against "the fact that American women are kept from growing to their full capacities," a handicap that she called "the **problem** that has no name" (*The Feminine Mystique*, 1963). Yet many educationists of the late twentieth century and the new millennium have become convinced that educational technology and "**problem**-based learning" (emphases on "**problem**-solving" and "**problem**-finding") will solve all of our **problems**—in spite of B. F. Skinner's warning that "the real **problem** is not whether machines think but whether men do" (*Contingencies of Reinforcement*, 1969).

PUBERTY

(noun) the stage of human physical development when sexual reproduction becomes possible

"Pop music trends come and go," observed a recent music review in the *Boston Globe*, "but **puberty** never goes out of style." In terms of the English language, **puberty**, the noun, has been in style since it was introduced in 1382 by John Wycliffe.

A direct borrowing from the Latin Bible, **puberty** (*pubertas*) occurs in one of Malachi's admonitions to remain faithful to the Lord. And marital fidelity, "between you and the wife of your **puberty** [pubertee]" (Malachi 2:14), is one of the fundamental ways that godly devotion must be expressed. In this context, **puberty** refers literally to the time when a male youth comes of age and takes his first bride in the marriage bed. (The Latin root of the noun is *puer*, "boy.")

Ironically, with the onset of the new millennium, there's been a growing awareness that for *girls*, **puberty** has begun to occur much earlier than ever before. (The cover story of the October 20, 2000, issue of *Time* reads, "Early **Puberty**, Why Girls Are Growing Up Faster.") But by all counts, **puberty** for both boys *and* girls continues to get an equal share in the titles of the survival guides for adolescents (and their parents). On occasion, however, the noun gets pushed to the limits (*Cosmic Puberty: From Atoms to Consciousness*) or honed for effect, as in this July 2000 headline from a *Washington Post* movie review: "Here's What I Learned from *X-Men*: **Puberty** Is Hell on Mutants."

Q

QUICK AND THE DEAD

everybody, alive and deceased

Although this phrase first appears in Wycliffe's 1382 translation of the Bible as "quick and dead," it becomes the more familiar **quick and the dead** in the 1388 Wycliffite version of 1 Peter. There, Peter warns the congregation not to fall prey to "the sins of the flesh," for those who do so "shall give reason to him, that is ready to deem the **quick and the dead** [quyke and the deed]" (1 Peter 4:5). It is a phrase frequently used in sermons as well as being part of the Apostles' Creed.

Let us hastily explain that "quick" in this phrase does not refer to speed, as it does in the humorist Ogden Nash's question, "How did I get so old so quick?" Instead, the word refers to what's vital or alive, as in the related phrase "cut to the quick." ("To quicken" refers to the stage of pregnancy in which the movement of the fetus can be felt.) In *On the Infinite Universe and Worlds*, a 1584 work of philosophy, the controversial Italian philosopher Giordano Bruno noted the power of contradictions: "It is Unity that doth enchant me. By her power I am free though thrall, happy in sorrow, rich in poverty, and quick even in death." In the final act of *Hamlet*, Laertes calls out from his sister Ophelia's grave, "Now pile your dust upon the quick and dead" (V.i.251).

*The **Quick and the Dead**, a 1995 western starring Gene Hackman and Sharon Stone, was described this way in a recent cable showing: "A cowgirl enters a quick-draw contest to get revenge on an outlaw in a town called Redemption." And

134

another variant of the phrase occurs as the title of a history of "combat point firing," *Quick or Dead*. By contrast, however, in a poignant 1946 speech to the United Nations, the statesman Bernard Baruch urged the world's leaders to contemplate seriously the implications of entering the atomic age. "My fellow citizens of the world," Baruch began, "we are here to make a choice between the **quick and the dead**. . . . We must elect world peace or world destruction."

QUIET

(adjective) making no sound or noise; not moving or acting

For having such a reticent reputation, **quiet** has made its wordly presence known in English as a noun, verb, adverb, and adjective, but it is Wycliffe's version of Paul's First Letter to the Thessalonians that introduces the adjective into the written language. (The other parts of speech were later nonbiblical coinages, although Coverdale was one of the first to use the adverb *quietly*.)

In his instructions to the faltering faithful of Thessalonica, Paul reinforces the need to abstain from immorality, to live "quietly" (as the Revised Standard Version translates it): "We pray . . . that you be **quiet** and do your need" (1 Thessalonians 4:11). The connotations here follow from the adjective's Latin cognate, *quietus*, the participial form of the verb *quiescere*, "to be at rest [with oneself]"—or as Wycliffe's Paul coins it elsewhere, to lead a "**quiet** and peaceable life" (1 Timothy 2:2). Another sense of this **quiet** space can be found in *coy* and *while*, both of which belong to **quiet**'s family tree.

But over the years **quiet** has been neither coy nor restful. Shakespeare, for example, turned dozens of phrases with its help ("**quiet** as a lamb" [*King John*, IV.i.79] and "Truth hath a **quiet** breast" [*Richard II*, I.iii.96]), as did Wordsworth in "It Is a Beauteous Evening" ("a beauteous evening . . . as **quiet** as a nun"). More recently, novelists have used it effectively in the titles of their work: *All **Quiet** on the Western Front* (1929) by Erich Maria Remarque and *The **Quiet** American* (1955) by Graham Greene. However, as the title of a recent study of emphysema made clear (*The **Quiet** Killer: Emphysema/Chronic Obstructive Pulmonary Disease*), **quiet** can also be powerful without being peaceful. Nonetheless, the American poet Theodore Roethke yearned "for the imperishable **quiet** at the heart of form" in "The Longing" (1964).

R

REAP THE WHIRLWIND

earn trouble or difficulty from earlier actions

In Wycliffe's 1382 translation of the Bible, the prophet Hosea uses this phrase for the first time in English. He warns of God's bitter retribution to an ungrateful Israel, exclaiming, "For they shall sow wind, and **reap whirlwind** [repe whirlwynd]" (Hosea 8:7). (Some two hundred years later, the translators of the Geneva Bible added the more familiar article "the.")

Hosea's angry words have long been echoed by other writers wanting to warn others about extreme consequences for thoughtless actions. A frequent title of political columns and vituperative speeches, the phrase is also found in at least a dozen fiction and nonfiction book titles—on subjects ranging from Nkrumah's rule of Ghana to World War II bomber forces. Most recently a spy thriller has been named after it, *Reap the Whirlwind* by Douglas De Bono (2001), and a new harvest of titles have grown up around it—minus the "whirl": *Reap the Savage Wind*, *Reap the Bitter Wind*, and take your pick of either the *South* or the *East Wind*.

And in a rather long-winded *Tampa Tribune* editorial about "environmentalism that borders on absurdity," the claim was made that "California **reaps the whirlwind** and Florida ignores the storm warning" (June 30, 2001).

ROOT OF ALL EVIL

basis or cause of sin

You're familiar with the saying "Money is the **root of all evil**"? If you are, you may be surprised that the proper saying says something else entirely. The King James Version puts it this way: "For the love of money is the root of all evil: which while some coveted after, they have erred from the faith, and pierced themselves through with many sorrows" (1 Timothy 6:10). However, it is Wycliffe's version of the Bible that first plants this deep-rooted phrase into the English language.

Although the shortened form is more popular, the longer actually expresses a different concern. It is not money itself but a person's attitude toward money that leads to "sinfulness." The Vulgate Bible's Latin wording is "radix enim omnium malorum est cupiditas" (literally "the root of all evil is *cupiditas*," which Wycliffe translates as "covetyse"). This in turn was quoted by Wycliffe's contemporary, Geoffrey Chaucer, in *The Canterbury Tales* as simply "Radix malorum est cupiditas." Nevertheless, whether it's "greed," "covetousness," or "cupidity," the emphasis is on the excessive love of money—or anything material for that matter.

ROSE-COLORED

(adjective) the pinkish red or light crimson of a rose

William Tyndale is the first to use this compound adjective in English—but not through the "**rose-colored** spectacles" (or Americanized "glasses") of Victorian optimism popularized (and coined) by Thomas Hughes in his *Tom Brown at Oxford* (1861). For Tyndale, **rose-colored** is the hue of the "beast" upon which sits the Great Whore of the Book of Revelation. According to John, "I saw a woman sit upon a **rose colored** beast" (Revelation 17:3).

A generation after Tyndale, Shakespeare was creating characters who were "rose lipped" and "rose cheeked," but the King James translators decided against Tyndale's coinage in favor of the sinful-sounding "scarlet-colored," which has been the accepted term ever since. (However, over the years everything from algae to spoonbills has been labeled **rose-colored**.)

The Latin word Jerome chose for this passage, *coccinus* (from *coccus*, "berry"), translates as "scarlet," and in a peculiar mismatch of meaning, the optimism of **rose-colored**ness has been colored over by the semantics of disease: *coccus* ("seed" or "berry" and its bacteriumlike shape) has become the combining form for names of a variety of diseases (*streptococcus*).

S

SALT Of THE EARTH

individual(s) of great worthiness; "real" people

The Bible is peppered with references to "salt," and **salt of the earth** is perhaps the most memorable of those usages. Coined by Wycliffe in his 1382 version of the Sermon on the Mount, the phrase actually is rooted in an earlier biblical translation, the *Lindisfarne Gospel* (c. A.D. 950), where it still reflects the influence of Germanic inflections: "thee sint salt eorthes." Wycliffe translates it into the word order of early Modern English: "ye are the **salt of the earth** [erthe]" (Matthew 5:13), Jesus tells his disciples. (Wycliffe's contemporary, Geoffrey Chaucer, used the same phrase about four years later in *The Canterbury Tales*.)

But in the Bible, salt is much more than a figure of speech or a condiment. According to *Harper's Bible Dictionary*, "in the *Talmud* 'salt' symbolizes the *Torah*, for as a world cannot exist without salt, so it cannot without the *Torah*." Similarly, as a preservative, *salt* became metaphorically associated with friendship and the "covenant" between God and His people. The Book of Mark, in fact, ends with a strong reference to this union: "See that ye have salt in yourselves and have peace among yourselves, one with another" (Mark 9:50; Tyndale's translation).

In recent times the phrase has become as commonplace as salt itself. A recent novel by Jack Olsen took the phrase as its title (as do at least thirty other books). The last cut on the Rolling Stones' classic *Beggars Banquet* album (1968) is **"Salt** of the Earth"; because of the song's rousing celebration of everyday heroes, Mick Jagger and Keith Richards performed it when they appeared at a benefit concert in 2001 for the families of firefighters and police victimized by the terrorist attacks of September 11. *Salt of the Earth* is also the title of a movie blacklisted during the 1950s Cold War era. Directed by Herbert Biberman, the film revealed the horrific oppression of Mexican American miners and their battle to overcome that degradation.

But George Bernard Shaw held on to the biblical roots when he wrote in *Androcles and the Lion*, "They may not be the **salt of the earth**, these Philistines, but they are the substance of civilization." (The play was first performed in 1912.)

SCAPEGOAT

(noun) a person, group, or thing that is blamed for the mistakes, crimes, or sins of others

A combination of the aphetic form of *escape*, which was used frequently by Shakespeare and others, and *goat*, Tyndale's memorable coinage (1530) names one of two goats used in the Day of Atonement ritual. By contrast, in his 1382 translation, Wycliffe prefers the prosaic phrase "goat that shall be sent out."

In Leviticus, the God of the Old Testament counsels Moses on how Aaron is to select two goats—one that will be sacrificed as a burnt offering to the Lord, and a second goat that will "escape" sacrifice and be set free into the wilderness, symbolically to bear the sins of the people: "And Aaron cast lots over the two goats: one lot for the Lord, and another for a **scapegoat** [scape-goote]" (Leviticus 16:8). A further enrichment of this story unfolds in the Revised Standard Version, where the idea of the **scapegoat** is modified so that the spared goat is sent to Azazel, the Hebrew name for an evil, monster-like creature that lives in the wild. In that translation, **scapegoat** becomes "the other [goat] for Azazel." (Isaac Asimov titled a collection of his stories *Azazel.*)

But as the ritualized meaning of **scapegoat** declined, the now-familiar personified meaning was in the ascendant. By the mid-nineteenth century, all the sin and blame that had been purified by symbolic transfer was henceforth projected onto anyone or anything targeted as a foil for another's crimes or mistakes. By the 1940s, **scapegoat** had become a verb (not surprisingly in the *Journal of Abnormal and Social Psychology*), and by the 1960s, an *ism* (**scapegoatism**). In a recent survey of newspapers published during a two-year period, **scapegoat** turned up in at least a thousand citations, suggesting that Tyndale's invention (as well as the practice) is still roaming free—but not, we presume, in the **Scapegoat** Wilderness Area of northwestern Montana.

SCRAPE

(verb) to remove or rub over by moving across a surface, usually with something sharp

Satan tests Job's loyalty to God by first destroying all of his children and material possessions. When that fails to break his will, confident in Job's steadfast devotion, God gives Satan permission to afflict the only thing that Job has left, his body. Assured of his own success, Satan then "smites" Job "with the worst stinking bleyne ['pustules'] from the sole of the foot to the top; the which with a shard **scraped** away" (Job 2:8).

That Job got out of this **scrape** has become proverbial; that Wycliffe came up with this coinage is not so well known. Returning to his English roots, Wycliffe utilizes the Old English verb *screpan*, which shares the Indo-European root *sker* in common with *sharp*, *shear*, and *scorpion*. Not that he is **scraping** the bottom of the barrel, but this first usage remains only one of four times that **scrape** occurs throughout the Bible.

Although the noun form was a later eighteenth-century addition to the language, **scrape**, like a utility knife, has been both versatile and creepy. We can "just **scrape** by" or "**scrape** together enough money to retire," but when someone **scrapes** his or her fingernails across a chalk board, we're reminded that Satan might have had a better alternative for testing Job's mettle.

SEASHORE

(noun) the land adjacent to the sea

The perpetual tongue twister "She sells seashells by the **seashore**" has been one of the more memorable ways by which Tyndale's coinage has survived in the English language. Others include the inescapable real estate advertisement, obligatory motel name, and the official names of the many scenic **seashores** along the coastal United States (Cape Cod, Cape Hatteras, Gulf Islands, etc.).

However, the first time **seashore** is found in the written record is in Tyndale's New Testament (1526). Paul in his Epistle to the Hebrews makes a sustained and convincing argument for the necessity of sustained faith. As one of his supporting examples, he cites the faith of Abraham and his wife Sarah, who in their old age were able to conceive and give birth to descendants "so many in multitude . . . as the sand of the **seashore** [sea shore] which is innumerable" (Hebrews 11:12), an analogy that calls to mind imagery from a recent Christmas-season headline in the *Washington Post*, "Shoppers Turned Out like Lemmings Hellbent for the **Seashore**."

SEER

(noun) one who can foresee or divine the future; clairvoyant

Exclusively an Old Testament noun, **seer** first appears in written English in the wrong place. As a coinage in Wycliffe's Bible, it's found in 1 Kings 9:9 (where the *OED* locates it); however, all subsequent translators edited together the Books of Kings and the Books of Samuel such that Wycliffe's 1 Kings is now 1 Samuel. Even in context, **seer** is somewhat out of place. It occurs in a passage that reads like an in-text footnote, glossing the distinction between the dated usage of **seer** and the more current preference for *prophet*.

The story line picks up with Saul and "his child" ("servant" in later versions) searching the countryside for his father's stray asses. Realizing that it's getting late and that people would begin to worry about them, the child suggests they go to a nearby village to seek help from a "man of God" who lives there: "Cometh, and go we to the **seer**; forsooth he, that today is said a prophet, sometime was called a **seer**" (1 Kings/1 Samuel 9:9). In other words, by that time **seer** was out of date as a term for the prophetic character, who had become identified with the spokesperson of God.

It's interesting to speculate about Wycliffe's choice of words here. Did he go to the Old English *seon* ("to see") for effect? Would **seer**, like its Old Testament counterpart, have been read literally as an "old" (non-Latin) word? Whatever his motives, the word has been left in place for centuries. (Luther used *Seher*, the Germanic first cousin of the Old English noun.)

The staying power of the word matches the perennial human preoccupation with the paranormal. Today the **seer** is someone who claims to foresee the future but does not claim to speak the prophetic word of God. As Emerson secularized it in his 1838 "Divinity School Address": "If utterance is

147

denied, the thought lies like a burden on the man. Always the **seer** is the sayer." Among those who've been given that title (that is, in titles of books about them) are William Blake, Walt Whitman, Edgar Allan Poe, Jeanne Dixon, Edgar Cayce, and the preeminent photographer Alfred Stieglitz. *The Seer* was also the title of a 1985 hit song and album recorded by the British rock group Big Country.

SEVENTY TIMES SEVEN

large number; beyond simple counting

Forgiveness, according to the New Testament, should never be in short supply. In fact, Peter asks Jesus how often he should be expected to forgive his brother for sinning. When Peter wonders whether seven times would be enough, Jesus replies, "I say not unto thee seven times: but **seventy times seven** times" (Matthew 18:22). Tyndale is the first to count this phrase among the biblical coinages written in English. Wycliffe's translation, by contrast, relies on a now obsolete Old Scottish word, *syth* ("compensation"): "seventy syths seventy sithis."

The result of that multiplication is not meant to reach a specific number. Rather, the arithmetic is supposed to suggest a far higher "product" than simple counting can produce. In other words, the practice of forgiving should not be limited to a certain number of occasions. But the expression most likely also carried with it larger symbolic power. According to *Harper's Bible Dictionary*, for example, the number *seven* was considered "the Hebrew sacred number par excellence." Among its potential **seventy times seven** connotations, it numbers the days of creation, the Sabbath, and the number of sentences Jesus spoke from the cross.

On the other hand, seventy is not always thought of as being such a large figure. Consider the wry comment of the American jurist Oliver Wendell Holmes Jr. at the age of ninety, when he spied an attractive younger woman: "Oh, to be seventy again!"

SEX

(noun) either of two divisions, male or female, into which humans and other species are divided

For some people, to have **sex** in the Bible in the first place (Genesis!) is unthinkable, but in his 1382 translation, Wycliffe, appealing to the venerable authority of Jerome's Latin Bible (*sexus*), does it. It occurs in the story of Noah and the Ark as God commands Noah to fill his ship with every living animal, two by two, "that male **sex** and female live with you" (Genesis 6:19). However, the Englishing of **sex** was short-lived. Six years later, in their revision of that first text, Wycliffe's followers replace **sex** with a four-letter word: *kind*. According to Strong's *Exhaustive Concordance of the Bible*, **sex** never occurs again in the Bible.

But it gets talked about in hundreds of ways. Anne Morrow Lindbergh, for example, observed in *Locked Rooms and Open Doors* (1974) that "People talk about **sex** as though it hopped about by itself, like a frog!" The reason for this, as Shirley MacLaine pointed out eleven years later in *Dancing in the Light*, might be that "**sex** is hardly about **sex**." Nevertheless, even a brief fling with a dictionary opened to the *s* word reveals its almost universal **sex** appeal: "**sex**ploitation" of the "fairer **sex**" (or is it the "weaker **sex**"?), because someone's been perceived as a "**sex** object" or "**sex** toy" or a member of the "third **sex**," might not involve a "**sex** offender," but usually points to some form of "**sex**ism" and the obvious need for either a stronger program in "**sex** education," or the intervention of a "**sex** therapist."

Incidentally, as a term for sexual intercourse ("to have **sex**"), **sex** was a late comer, first appearing in D. H. Lawrence's *Pansies* (1929).

SHIBBOLETH

(noun) any word, phrase, or pronunciation indicative of a person's origin; a password or otherwise distinctive catchword adopted by a unique group of people

In the Old Testament, as we explained in this book's introduction, the Book of Judges contains the earliest of spy stories. As Wycliffe tells it, when the conquered Ephraimites try to pass themselves off as the conquering Gileadites, the pretenders are asked to pronounce the Gileadite word *shibboleth* ("an ear of corn"), but because of their language idiosyncrasies, they can produce only the mispronunciation "sibboleth": They asked him [to] say . . . **shibboleth** [shebboleth], that is to mean an ear [of corn], the which answered sibboleth [sebolech]" (Judges 12:6). In this case, it was a dead giveaway, and they were summarily executed. (The modern spelling appears for the first time in the King James translation.)

Today the English use of **shibboleth** for a code word or telling example of insider jargon has moved far beyond its biblical origin. Newcomers to the nation's capital, for instance, can be readily identified by the **shibboleth** of "Silver Spring," a Maryland suburb of Washington often mispronounced as a plural, "Silver Springs." An episode in the 1970s cop series *Kojak* hinged on Theo Kojak hearing a criminal who was pretending to be a New Yorker mispronounce "Houston Street." (As any bona fide resident of the Big Apple knows, the street's name is not pronounced like that of the city in Texas—the "ou" sounds like "ow.") And native speakers of French, who don't have the "th" sound in their vocal repertoire because it is pronounced as a hard "t," would be in deep trouble like the Ephraimites, if their safety depended on being able to correctly pronounce **shibboleth**, regardless of the first syllable.

SIN OF THE FATHERS

evil attributed to ancestors; fault of forefathers

In Tyndale's 1530 version of Exodus, as God begins to spell out the Ten Commandments, he forbids the making of any "similitude" or **"graven image"** (see entry) of Himself: "See that thou neither bow thyself unto them neither serve them," the Lord commands, "for I the Lord thy God, am a jealous God, and visit the **sin of the fathers**" (Exodus 20:5). Earlier, Wycliffe had opted for "wickedness of the fathers," and later, the King James translators decided on "iniquities." Not until about a hundred years after Tyndale's Bible, however, in *The Book of Common Prayer*, would that commandment be expressed as the more familiar plural **sins of the fathers**.

How long will the **sin of the fathers** be held against their descendants? The passage in Exodus suggests a long grudge, "unto the third and fourth generation of them that hate me."

According to the sixteenth edition of *Bartlett's Familiar Quotations*, the idea had widespread representation in ancient and Renaissance thought. Euripides, the Greek playwright, noted in *Phrixus*, "The gods visit the sins of the fathers upon the children," and Horace agreed in his Roman *Odes*: "For the sins of your fathers you, though guiltless, must suffer." In *The Merchant of Venice*, William Shakespeare preferred the singular form for the parent in noting, "The sins of the father are to be laid upon the children" (III.v.1–2).

A 2002 television movie about the effects of a 1963 hate crime on the next generation was titled *Sins of the Father*, starring Ving Rhames; according to its ads, "Thirty years ago a tragic event shocked the nation. Now, one son must find the courage to tell the truth and bring his father to justice." An earlier 1991 telefilm starring Elizabeth Montgomery as a controlling parent was released under the title *Sins of the Mother*.

In a recent episode of the CBS series *Everybody Loves Raymond*, however, the biblical phrase is given a humorous twist by Raymond's father, who argues, "The sins of the son shall not bother the father."

SLAUGHTER
(verb) to kill animals for food

When Coverdale's Isaiah rails at the revelry of an unfaithful Jerusalem, he uses the verb **slaughter** for the first time in English: "[the revelers] **slaughter** oxen, they kill sheep," then pledge to "eat and drink, for tomorrow we shall die" (Isaiah 22:13). Later in this same context, the noun form of **slaughter** appears in another phrase that has also become familiar to most readers of the King James Bible: "[to be brought] as a lamb to the **slaughter**" (53:7).

From an Old Norse root, *slatr*, with ties to the Old English *sleuht*, **slaughter** is related to *slay* and *slain* and shares in the legacy of a family history that has been horrific—what the poet Kenneth Patchen called "the footsteps of this **slaughtered** age" (in "Let Us Have Madness"). Although as early as 1300 the noun was also used to describe the killing of people *and* animals, it was not until the beginning of the seventeenth century that the verb was used to refer to **slaughtering** people. Today, even a very limited search on LEXIS-NEXIS turns up more than a thousand citations for **slaughter**, and those are recorded for only the previous month. But it's the haunting title of Kurt Vonnegut Jr.'s 1969 novel *Slaughterhouse-Five* that reminds us of the human capacity for human carnage.

SODOM AND GOMORRAH

biblical cities; centers of wickedness

Lot, the nephew of Abraham, is allowed to choose the land where he and his family will live. Lot lifts up his eyes, Wycliffe's narrator of Genesis says, and sees that the plain of Jordan is full of water—"before the Lord destroyed **Sodom and Gommorah** [gomor]" (Genesis 13:10). Although after the fact, this is the first appearance of these two infamous cities in written English. (The more familiar spelling debuts in the King James Version.)

What causes those two cities on the plain of Jordan to be demolished? Chapter 19 of Genesis tells the story of two angels who visit Lot at Sodom and are nearly molested by the inhabitants. The angels warn Lot and his family to flee the two cities while they can without looking back (see **pillar of salt**). According to the account, "Then the Lord rained upon Sodom and upon Gomorrah brimstone and fire from the Lord out of heaven" (Genesis 19:24).

This cautionary tale is remembered throughout the Bible. In the King James version of Matthew, for instance, Jesus sends forth his disciples to preach and tells them to avoid any inhospitable urban audience. "It shall be more tolerable," Jesus warns, "for the land of **Sodom and Gomorrah** in the day of judgment, than for that city" (Matthew 10:15).

The wickedness of the first city is memorialized in English by the toponymous words *sodomite* for a male prostitute and *sodomy*. There is no word *gomorrahy*, but the second city has an equally bad reputation. For instance, an article in *The Guardian* (London) expressed relief that "the commercial Gomorrah that is Valentine's Day is over" (February 18, 2002).

Not all literary allusions to these cities, however, find these places shocking to modern sensibilities. A 1704 essay by Thomas Brown on London taverns pointed out, "A Tavern is a little Sodom, where as many Vices are daily practic'd, as ever were known in the great one." Dostoyevsky, the nineteenth-century Russian novelist, also weighed the power of Sodom in a passage of *The Brothers Karamazov*, translated by Constance Garnett: "What to the mind is shameful is beauty and nothing else to the heart. Is there beauty in Sodom? Believe me, that for the immense mass of mankind beauty is found in Sodom. Did you know that secret? The awful thing is that beauty is mysterious as well as terrible. God and devil are fighting there, and the battlefield is the heart of man."

The two cities hit the big screen in 1963 with ***Sodom and Gomorrah***, starring Stewart Granger, and by the new millennium they had become the butt of one of Jay Leno's jokes— one of "The Week's Best Late-Night Laughs" listed in a recent edition of the *Toronto Sun*: "Bill Clinton is visiting Israel this week. He gave a speech yesterday and then he went to his two favorite cities in the Holy Land—**Sodom and Gomorrah**" (January 27, 2002).

SORCERER

(noun) one who practices magic or the secret arts; wizard

To say that the source of Harry Potter's **sorcerer** is Tyndale's New Testament (1525) is not to suggest a new plotline for another volume in that series but to identify the noun **sorcerer** as a biblical coinage. It materializes in the Book of Acts as Saul, Barnabas, and John spread the gospel to the people of Cyprus. When they have "gone throughout the isle" and arrive in Paphos, "they [find] a certain **sorcerer** [sorserer] . . . who withstood them" (Acts 13:6).

Stemming from the Latin root *sors* ("lot," "share," "sort," and their implicit connections to fate and chance), this first appearance of **sorcerer** is the only time that the singular form of the noun occurs in the Bible. The older *sorcery* (1300) and *sorceress* (Chaucer's coinage in 1384) also turn up only once in both the Old and the New Testaments. (The plural forms of all three occur only about a half-dozen times combined.)

If Harry is the current extension of Paul Dukas's *Sorcerer's Apprentice* (1897) and its alter ego, Disney's *Fantasia* (1940), then with the 1998 publication of his story, he landed in good recent company with Sir Isaac Newton (*Newton: The Last Sorcerer*, a 1999 biography) and with Nikola Tesla (*Tesla: The Modern Sorcerer*, another biography published the same year).

SPRINKLER

(noun) a device used to spray or otherwise distribute water

Animal Ambassadors, one of the twenty-three floats awarded a trophy in the 2002 Tournament of Roses Parade, was sponsored by the Rain Bird **Sprinkler** Manufacturing Corporation—an honor that surely made the members of the National Fire **Sprinkler** Association very proud. But honor is not in the Old Testament picture when this noun makes its English debut in Coverdale's Book of Jeremiah (1535). In the course of the capture and burning of Jerusalem in 587 B.C., one of Nebuchadnezzar's generals loots and burns everything inside the Temple, including "the cauldrons, shawls . . . **sprinklers**, spoons, and all the brass vessel[s]" (Jeremiah 52:18).

Coverdale's choice of **sprinkler** to denote a vessel for holy water, however, is not without precedent. A hundred and fifty years earlier, with the same holy-water font in mind, Wycliffe uses the noun *sprinkle* for the first time in English: "The little **sprinkle** [sprynkil] of hyssop wetted in blood" (Exodus 12:22).

Also, **sprinkler** belongs to the Old English/Germanic tradition still evident in the German noun *Sprenkel* and to the earlier Indo-European root that generated *spark* and *speckle*. In a remarkable example of linguistic self-nullification, the contemporary version of a **sprinkler** is an apparatus designed to extinguish a spray of flying sparks.

And even though **sprinkler** is one of a kind in the Bible

(appearing only this one time), nowadays lawn **sprinklers** and fire **sprinklers** are marketed in an endless variety of styles. In fact, even a Pink Flamingo Garden **Sprinkler** is now available online (at www.uptownflamingo.com).

STARGAZER

(noun) one who studies the stars; astrologer

True, the venerable "three wise men from the east" may be the most celebrated gazers of a biblical star, but in the Geneva Bible (1560) Isaiah claims the distinction of being the first to use the word **stargazer**. Referring to the fall of Babylon, he personifies that city as one who "felt secure in your wickedness," and now challenges her "astrologers, the **stargazers** [starre gasers] and prognosticators [to] stand up [and save you from these things]" (Isaiah 47:13).

A compression of Wycliffe's earlier "those who behold the stars," **stargazer** was retained in the King James Version of this passage and now appears dozens of times throughout the entire Bible. It also has become the name of a fish that has eyes on top of its head (*uranoscopus scaber*), a race horse that's in the habit of throwing *back* its head, a film production company (**Stargazer** Productions), a senior women's dance troupe from suburban Atlanta, and, of course, the perduring daydreamer, astrologer, and amateur astronomer. In a recent news story, "veteran **stargazers**" were sought after for their expertise regarding the November 2001 Leonids meteor shower.

STIFF-NECKED

(adjective) obstinate, haughty, self-righteous

Try to imagine what Tyndale would have thought of American football ritual and iconography—especially that genuflection-inducing move called the "stiff arm." For when he coined the adjective **stiff-necked** in 1526, he obviously wasn't thinking about necks nearly paralyzed from the strain of watching the Super Bowl on television, but he did have a sense of someone being a "pain in the neck," namely those resistant to the spread of the gospel. Recounting the words of the Old Testament God, Tyndale's Stephen derides those nonbelievers as "You **stiffnecked** [stiffenecked] and of uncircumcised hearts and ears" (Acts 7:51).

Today **stiff-necked**, as a synonym for haughtiness, is found in dozens of passages throughout the Bible but rarely encountered in popular usage. The closest we get to that original meaning is by association—when we refer to someone who turns his or her nose up in self-righteous indignation. Nevertheless, we're all equal when it comes to physical pain, and a "stiff neck" (coined in 1893) can humble even the most obnoxiously self-important heretic.

STRANGER IN A STRANGE LAND

a person in unfamiliar territory

Frequently the Bible's narration will pause to explain the meaning of a name being given to a place or a newborn. In Exodus, for instance, Moses takes Zipporah as his wife after he flees from Pharaoh to the land of Midian. And it is in Tyndale's translation of this verse that the coinage first appears: Zipporah "bare a son, and he called him Gerson: for he said. I have been a **stranger in a strange land**" (Exodus 2:22).

The poetic phrase **stranger in a strange land** sounds redundant, but it is the meaning of the name "Gerson," the firstborn son of Moses. Later (in the King James translation of the same book), Moses announces a slightly varied definition for a variant spelling of the name: "the name of the one was Gershom; for he said, I have been an alien in a strange land" (Exodus 18:3). The word *alien* appears only five places in the King James Version, but its translators were obviously no strangers to its synonym *stranger*, which appears more than 125 times.

Sophocles, in the ancient Greek play *Oedipus at Colonus*, offered a similar expression, which was translated into English by Robert Fitzgerald as "stranger in a strange country." Robert A. Heinlein picked up *Stranger in a Strange Land* to title his popular 1961 science fiction novel, and columnists have also favored the familiar expression. In a 2000 edition of *The Ragan Report* on business communication, the word columnist Alden Wood employed it to warn against misreading

"Gunga Din" for "gung ho." In the cleverly titled column "Typochondriac," Professor Wood provided this mnemonic moral: "When you are a **stranger in a strange land**, be sure you grok the talk."

Usually, however, it is the first noun in the phrase that changes. For instance, in a 1999 Baen Books paperback, Harry Turtledove's Hugo-winning science fiction 1993 story of "Down in the Bottomlands" is described on the back cover as "Lawyer in a Strange Land."

SUFFER FOOLS GLADLY

show patience to the undeserving

Tyndale's translation of one of Paul's letters was the source of this phrase in written English. In his Second Letter to the church at Corinth, Paul gives the members an object lesson against foolishness by pretending to speak like a fool. "For ye **suffer fools gladly**," he says, tongue pressed firmly in cheek, "because that ye yourselves are wise" (2 Corinthians 11:19).

Paul's sarcasm uses the verb *suffer* in the sense of "put up with" or "endure." In an earlier passage in Mark, by contrast, the same verb is employed to suggest "allow" or "permit," as in the displeasure of Jesus when young children are kept from him. "Suffer the little children to come unto me," he says, "and forbid them not. For of such is the kingdom of God" (Mark 10:14).

Modern usage tends to prefer the meaning of "endure,"

as in the suffering of pain. In the 1848 novel *Vanity Fair*, William Makepeace Thackeray selected that sense when commenting on a character that "He suffered his grandmother with a good-humored indifference." The full expression is found in the May 2000 issue of *National Geographic*, where Priit J. Vesilind wrote, "Iceland remains a community of pragmatists that does not **suffer fools gladly**, and its modern Scandinavian veneer barely hides a Viking heart." Although the expression has developed into a stock phrase, it is now primarily used in the negative, complimenting those who are least able to **suffer fools gladly**.

T

THIRTY PIECES OF SILVER

payment or wages; price of betrayal

Judas Iscariot, the disciple who delivers Jesus into the hands of the chief priests, expects money from them for the act of betrayal. According to Tyndale's narrator, "And they covenanted with him for **thirty pieces of silver**" (Matthew 26:14). This is the first written use of that phrase in English, but both the expression and the price tag circulate like currency throughout the Bible. In the next chapter of Matthew in the King James Version, for instance, Judas realizes what he has done and repents, returning "the **thirty pieces of silver** to the chief priests and elders" (Matthew 27:3). (Here both Tyndale and Wycliffe preferred "plates of silver.") Judas hangs himself, and the priests use their returned **blood money** (see entry) to buy the potter's field as a burial ground for strangers.

The same sum of money also appears in an earlier passage of the Bible. When an Old Testament prophet seeks compensation from the people, he learns that "they weighed for my price **thirty pieces of silver**" (Zechariah 11:12), a trivial amount that the Lord finds offensive. Unlike the King James Version as it appears here, and anticipating Tyndale's preferences elsewhere, Wycliffe's translation of this passage opts for "plates" [platis]. But instead of "plates" and "pieces," the market value of silver also shifts. When Joseph is sold into Egyptian slavery, his brothers accept only "twenty pieces of silver" (Genesis 38:28).

What would be the value today of those **thirty pieces of**

silver? According to *The Abingdon Bible Commentary*, it would be around $260. However, as David Hendin, author of *Guide to Biblical Coins*, has pointed out, "a single genuine shekel of Tyre, dating from the first century B.C. to the first century A.D., can be purchased from reputable ancient coin dealers for between around $250 to $1000 depending on condition."

THROUGH A GLASS DARKLY

seen unclearly or obscurely

Perhaps the most poetic passage in the New Testament is Paul's definition of love, delineated in the thirteenth chapter of 1 Corinthians. When Paul writes to the church members at Corinth about our limited ability as humans to understand the ways of God, he explains, "For now we see **through a glass darkly**: but then shall we see face to face: now I know in part: but then shall I know even as also I am known" (1 Corinthians 13:12).

This coinage of the Geneva Bible (1560), which was adopted by the King James translators, is found in Wycliffe as "in a mirror in darkness" and in Tyndale as "Now we see in a glass even in a dark speaking."

"Glass" and "mirror" may sound different, but in this case the meaning is the same: the roughly polished metallic surface that offers an imperfect reflection. In the same generation that the King James translators were working on the Bible, William Shakespeare was also using *glass* to mean a mirror, as in "the glass of fashion" in *Hamlet* (III.i.153). Nearly three centuries later, the British writer Lewis Carroll titled some of Alice's extraordinary adventures in Wonderland as *Through the Looking-Glass*.

At a Modern Language Association convention in 2001, a paper on the humor in the Canadian author Margaret Atwood's essays was titled "Through the Glass Lightly." More than a century earlier, Mark Twain gave the phrase his typical comic twist; in an 1895 essay about the American author James Fenimore Cooper, Twain commented on Cooper's limited literary abilities: "He saw nearly all things as through a glass eye, darkly."

TRANSfER

(verb) to convey or send from one person or place to another

Wycliffe's Ezekiel, speaking for the God of Israel, maps out the land that has been allotted to the Israelite tribes and warns them that "Neither the first fruits of the land shall be **transferred** [transferrid] for they are hallowed to the Lord" (Ezekiel 48:14). He uses the verb **transfer** for the first time in written English. But the coinage was short-lived, for six years later in the 1388 Wycliffite revised version of that passage, **transfer** has been translated as "translated," and **transfer** never again appears in the Old Testament. It occurs only once elsewhere in the Bible—in 1 Corinthians 4:6.

Another one of Wycliffe's direct borrowings from Jerome's Latin Bible, **transfer** is a literalization of the Latin verb *transferre*, which in turn compounds the prefix *trans* ("across") and the root *ferre* ("to bear or carry"). And not until the late seventeenth century does the meaning of the verb get **transferred** to the noun form.

Contemporary usage, however, has favored both parts of speech. In politics we always hope for a peaceful **transfer** of power, and students are continuously **transferring** into and out of schools, as educational psychologists promote the importance of learning **transfer**. We **transfer** money from one account to another as easily as we **transfer** bus lines. Even molecular biologists use the word to differentiate a **transfer** from a messenger RNA.

TREASURE

(verb) to put away or save anything considered valuable; to hoard

Wycliffe's 1382 Bible is literally a **treasure** chest of coinages, and the verb **treasure** really cashes in on that distinction. Not only does the verb form show up there for the first time, but so do a few other "firsts" that involve the word in a figurative sense ("treasure in heaven," "treasures of the house of the Lord").

The verb enters the written record in Isaiah when the prophet warns Hezekiah that eventually everything will be carried off to Babylon, including "all things that are in your house, and that your father has **treasured** [tresored]" (Isaiah 39:6). In contrast, the noun form predates this usage by about two hundred years and its sibling, *treasury*, predates the verb by nearly a hundred.

The source of the word, however, dates to the ancient Greeks and *thesauros*, their word for "a treasury or storehouse," and by association now our word for a word-hoard. Wycliffe, however, makes a straight transfer of the Latin equivalent (*thesaurus*) from Jerome's Bible into his English translation.

As both noun and verb, **treasure** can be found throughout the Bible as well as throughout that other **treasure** trove of English words, the works of Shakespeare, where among dozens of citations, a **treasure** hunt is required to find an example of the verb. It occurs only once: ". . . **treasure** thou some place / With beauty's **treasure**, ere it be self-killed" (Sonnet 6, lines 3–4). In another treasury of the English language, the works of John Milton, the verb is used in a passage that could have been written as the epigraph for the Bible itself: "A good book is the precious lifeblood of a master spirit, embalmed and **treasured** up on purpose to a life beyond life" (*Of Education*, 1644).

Television viewers will remember the verb's use in the 1977 finale of *The Mary Tyler Moore Show*. At the conclusion of that comedy series, Ed Asner, as the TV news producer Lou Grant, tells his tearful colleagues: "I **treasure** you people."

TWO-EDGED SWORD

doubly sharp weapon; blade that cuts both ways

Sword expressions are common throughout the Bible, but William Tyndale's rendition of Paul's Letter to the Hebrews gives the English language the term **two-edged sword** for the first time: "For the word of God is quick, and mighty in operation, and sharper than any **two-edged sword**" (Hebrews 4:12). A hundred and fifty years earlier Wycliffe chose instead to translate this cutting image as "tweyne eggid swerd." Although the word *sword* is first introduced to the written record with the tenth-century Anglo-Saxon epic *Beowulf*, both the New Testament and the Old Testament include hundreds of references to this weapon of war. Two of the most familiar are (in the King James Version) the reference to the "second coming" when nations "shall beat their swords into plowshares" (Isaiah 2:4) and Jesus' reminder to his followers that "all they that take the sword shall perish with the sword" (Matthew 26:52).

Usually, however, the **two-edged sword** is used metaphorically for an idea or issue that can be especially dangerous by cutting both ways, and it is sometimes described as "double-edged." The playwright John Fletcher wrote about a female character in the comedy *The Humorous Lieutenant* (c. 1620) that "She has two-edged eyes; they kill o' both sides." And recent Internet citations of **two-edged sword** describe its application to everything from tenure and inflation to information technology and law. During the 2000 presidential race, a Democratic pollster in Michigan was asked whether President Bill Clinton should be more visible in Al Gore's campaign strategy; the pollster replied: "He's a lot of help. He's a lot of hurt. He's the double-edged sword of American politics."

In her 1929 book-length essay, *A Room of One's Own*, Virginia Woolf sharpened that metaphor by commenting that "The beauty of the world has two edges, one of laughter, one of anguish, cutting the heart asunder."

UNCERTAINTY

(noun) the quality of being indeterminate or unsure

Among a litany of Polonius-like clichés, **uncertainty** enters the written record of the English language. In his First Letter to Timothy, Wycliffe's Paul preaches the ungodliness of riches and wealth, arguing that "we brought nothing into this world and can carry nothing out." And in order to "fight the good fight of faith," we must never forget that "the love of money is the root of all evil." Therefore, Paul concludes, we must not put all of our "hope in **uncertainty** [uncerteynte] of riches, but in quick [the living] God" (1 Timothy 6:17).

Two things are certain about this passage. One, **uncertainty** is a carryover from Jerome's Latin Vulgate (*incerto*), and two, this is both the first *and* the last time that the noun appears in the Bible. (Later versions use "uncertain riches.")

Why **uncertainty** keeps company with cliché is, well, uncertain, but Edith Hamilton's definition of the word offers some insight: "**Uncertainty** is the prerequisite for gaining knowledge and frequently the result as well" (*Spokesmen for God*, 1949). When the lay public refers to Heisenberg's **uncertainty** principle (1927), the **uncertainty** of that application usually has nothing to do with the scientific knowledge of quantum mechanics. Mark Twain, on the other hand, in a speech to the New England Society, could be uncertain just enough to assert the certainty of change: "one of the brightest gems of New England weather is the dazzling **uncertainty** of it" (1876).

UNDERGIRD

(verb) to secure or fasten from the bottom side

Unlike most of Wycliffe's newly Englished words, which are direct borrowings from Jerome's Latin, many of Tyndale's coinages are his own innovations, and **undergird** is a good example of his word making. The verb makes its first appearance in Paul's account of his sea voyage to Rome as a prisoner of the state. Caught in a violent storm, the prison ship takes safe harbor at Clauda, where attempts are made to strengthen it against the "tempestuous wind": "We . . . had much work to come by a boat, which they took up and used help, **undergirding** the ship" (Acts 27:17).

A hybrid of Old English words, **undergird** combines the preposition *under* and the verb *gyrdan*, and mirrors the Old Flemish word *ondergorden*, which in turn translates the Latin *subcingere* (*sub* ["under"] plus *cingere* ["to cinch"]) and ultimately reflects its New Testament Greek analogue. For this same passage, Wycliffe chooses to use only the verb form "girdyng," which also has an English biblical point of origin in the tenth-century *Lindisfarne Gospel*. A richly suggestive word, it has since provided us with *girders*, *girdles*, and *girth*.

Although this is the only passage in the Bible where **undergird** appears, it's commonly found in today's press when constitutional or moral issues are at stake. Typical in this regard are comments by Vermont's Senator Patrick Leahy in a recent *Baltimore Sun* article, where he criticized the Bush administration's military tribunal plan, pointing out that it "jeopardizes the separation of powers that **undergirds** our constitutional system" (November 29, 2001). And a similar claim on moral grounds was made in the *Ottawa Citizen*. Arguing against complaints that there's too much sex and violence in the Bible for children to be reading it, a "religion expert" emphasized that "[in the Bible] a moral framework **undergirds** the discussion of human immorality and inhumanity" (May 5, 2001).

UNDER THE SUN

on earth; in the world; beneath the sky

This heliocentric expression was already popular long before our modern understanding of the sun's place at the center of our solar system. The narrator of Ecclesiastes uses the phrase in a world-weary message: "The thing that hath been, it is that which shall be; and that which is done is that which shall be done: and there is no new thing **under the sun**" (Ecclesiastes 1:9). The end of that King James verse had already been expressed for the first time in written English in John Wycliffe's fourteenth-century Bible translation: "No thing **under the sunne** newe." With these words, the speaker dismisses any notion that pretends to be new or original.

Later in the same Old Testament book (King James Version), the narrator uses the same phrase in a happier saying: "Then I commended mirth, because a man hath no better thing **under the sun**, than to eat, and to drink, and to be merry" (Ecclesiastes 8:15; also see **eat, drink, and be merry**).

This prepositional phrase was expressed in Old English as "under sunnan" in a religious work that predates the year 1000. In *The Humorous Lieutenant* (c. 1620), the playwright John Fletcher also omitted the "the," commenting, "There fights no braver souldier under Sun, Gentlemen." More than two centuries later, Alfred Lord Tennyson tried a different preposition in "while we breathe beneath the sun" (*In Memoriam*, lxxv). Nowadays, though, the biblical phrase is still the most popular. A southern car dealer, for instance, advertises itself as "Number one **under the sun**," and Florida orange juice is sold as "The best start **under the sun**." The phrase has also been used to name a progressive California rock band, a travel insurance company in the United Kingdom, and a Web guide to sun safety.

Perhaps extended from this expression is the meteorological phrase *under the weather* to describe somebody who feels ill, but that euphemism has also been around a long time. As the Bible is quick to remind us, there's really nothing new **under the sun**.

UNGODLY

(adjective) having no reverence for a deity; irreligious, wicked

In Tyndale's 1526 version of Romans, Paul makes the gospel's case for justification by faith and the "new life" to be found in

Jesus, reminding the Roman faithful that "when we were yet weak, according to the time: Christ died for us which were **ungodly**" (Romans 5:6).

Another example of Tyndale's reluctance to follow the Latin of Wycliffe's (and Jerome's) Bible, **ungodly** appears for the first time in written English as a substitute for the Latin *impiis* ("impious"). Actually the adjective can be traced back to the Middle Dutch *ongodelijc* and other Scandinavian cognates, words that Wycliffe overlooked in favor of the Latinate "unpiteous." Four years before Tyndale's choice of **ungodly**, however, Luther translated the adjective in the opposite direction—not *un***godly** but "God*less*" (*Gottlose*).

But Tyndale's coinage has kept pace with the times. We don't complain about having to get up at a "godless" hour, but according to a recent survey, the **ungodly** hours we must awaken range from 3:00 A.M. to 8:00 A.M. Race-car drivers are described as traveling at "**ungodly** speeds," and superstar athletes receive "**ungodly** salaries." Or if you lived in Buffalo, New York, during the winter of 2001–2, "the **ungodly** winter weather" would have been the talk of the town. But the Bible is never too far away. In January 2002, the Catholic school board in Saskatoon, Alberta, "launched an investigation" into the Harry Potter books "after a group of parents argued the '**ungodly**' and 'evil' books should be banned from the classroom" (Montreal *Gazette*, January 23, 2002).

UPROAR

(noun) commotion or violent disturbance; tumultuous rising up of a body of people

Another one of Tyndale's coinages (1526) that attaches a preposition to a verb, **uproar** is actually the English variant of the Dutch word *oproer*, which exists in German as *Aufruhr* (the word Luther uses in his 1522 version). The noun appears in written English for the first time in the Book of Acts after Paul has been assaulted and arrested for preaching the gospel. The arresting officer asks Paul if he is "that Egyptian which before these days made an **uproar** [uproure] and led out into the wilderness about four thousand men?" (Acts 21:38).

Although today we'd probably use *uprising* in this context, **uproar**'s semantic field has far outgrown Tyndale's literal use of the word. For example, recent newspapers have informed us that there's an **uproar** over Medicare, Bush's military tribunal plan, Enron, property reassessments in Pittsburgh, hunters' slaughter of swans in Scotland, ferrets, and a plan for foreign languages on signs in Singapore. And there's this **uproar**ious headline from Australia, "**Uproar** over Shadowy Sex" (Queensland *Sunday Mail*, February 3, 2002)—a comment on the controversial staging of Sexpo 2002.

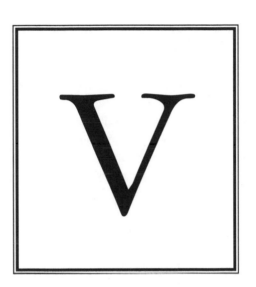

VIPER

(noun) any venomous snake or serpent; specifically
Pelias berus

Shipwrecked on Mileta as an escaped prisoner, Paul is greeted
by the native inhabitants who offer shelter and the warmth of
a fire: "And when Paul had gathered a bundle of sticks, and put
them into the fire, there came a **viper** out of the heat and leapt
on his hand" (Acts 28:3). Thus Tyndale introduces the literal
viper into written English, but he also handles the figurative **viper** for the first time as well. It occurs when John the
Baptist asks the Pharisees and Sadducees who've come to
watch him baptize, "O generation of **vipers**, who hath taught
you to flee from the vengeance to come?" (Matthew 3:7).

Straight out of the Latin of Jerome (*vipera*), the word
combines the Latin roots *vivus* ("living") and *parere* ("to
bear"), and literally means "to bear living," from the mistaken
belief that the **viper** does not lay eggs.

Today we have the Dodge **Viper** sports car, the **Viper**
F-16 attack jet, and "**Viper**-Man: The Reptilian Superhero."
In 1942 Philip Wylie titled his scathing attack on American
culture and society *Generation of Vipers*. And in the 1950s the
music of the British skiffle group the **Vipers** stung the musical
imagination of Paul McCartney. But the strangest incarnation
of all is what the noun meant in the late 1930s when someone
(usually a jazz musician) who smoked marijuana or other kinds
of "dope" was labeled a **viper**. The title of one of Sidney
Bechet's songs, in fact, is "**Viper** Mad."

VOICELESS

(adjective) incapable of speaking; mute

The Bible enshrines hundreds of "voices," but **voiceless** occurs only once and is never heard from again. In Coverdale's 1535 telling of the Book of Acts, an "Angel of the Lord" instructs Philip to help an Ethiopian official understand the writings of Isaiah. When Philip asks if the official understands what he read, we learn that "As a lamb **voiceless** [voycelesse] before his shearer so opened he not his mouth" (Acts 8:32). For Wycliffe and Tyndale, "dumb" was the adjective of choice for this passage, and after Coverdale, "dumb" was still the favorite of the King James and Revised Standard Versions.

However, the addition of the suffix *less* to another part of speech was neither an inappropriate nor an uncommon construction, especially in this case where the noun *voice* dates back to the early fourteenth century. Shakespeare, for example, coined *worthless, viewless,* and *noiseless* barely a generation after Coverdale. Most likely, the native Old English adjective *dumb* spoke to both the need for a biblical English and to the contextual needs of the passage. Whereas **voiceless** denotes the absence of sound, the earlier uses of "dumb" connote "not understanding," i.e., the interpretation of Isaiah's meaning.

But today **voiceless** speaks for the powerless. One of the strongest statements against political oppression, for instance, is Archbishop Oscar Romero's *Voice for the **Voiceless**: The Four Pastoral Letters and Other Statements* (1985). Again we hear it in *Voices of the **Voiceless**: Women, Justice, and Human Rights in*

Guatemala (1997) by Michelle Tooley, in *Tutu: Voice of the Voiceless* (1988) by Shirley DuBoulay, and an empire away in *Voiceless India* (1930) by Gertrude Sen.

VOICE OF THE TURTLE

bird's call; unexpected or long-unheard sound

Once the female narrator of Wycliffe's Song of Solomon hears her beloved calling her to him, she notices that the long winter has ended. "The flowers appear on the earth," she says, "the time of the singing of birds is come, and the **voice of the turtle** [vois of the turtil] is heard in our land" (Song of Solomon 2:12). And this is the first time the phrase is heard in the land of written English.

Do not expect, however, to hear a song from a terrapin or box turtle; the slow-moving creature in a shell is not the type of turtle whose voice is recognized in this poetic verse. Instead, "turtle" is short for *turtledove*, a cooing bird similar to a pigeon. This type of dove is known for its passivity and its affection for its mate. Although *turtledove* is used as a term of affection in the Bible, the bird is perhaps better known from the second verse of "The Twelve Days of Christmas," when "my true love gave to me two turtledoves and a partridge in a pear tree."

In modern times, the dramatist John Van Druten picked up the biblical phrase as a lyrical title for his 1943 romantic comedy. A recent New York revival of this wartime play received this unfavorable review in *Variety*: "*The **Voice of the Turtle*** is sounding pretty hoarse."

But on a happier note, the modern-day **voice of the turtle** has become multilingual. A quartet of musicians who specialize in the music of the Sephardim (the Jews of Spain) has taken the phrase as the name of their group, and two anthologies, one of Cuban stories and the other of American Indian literature, lead off with the title **"Voice of the Turtle."**

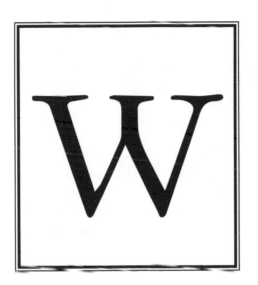

WORDY

(adjective) using too many words; verbose

Ironically, **wordy**, one of the wordiest words used by high school English teachers to comment on a student's writing ability, never appears in Shakespeare and only once occurs in the Bible—where in the beginning was the Word. Wycliffe's Job uses the adjective for the first time to describe how his "**wordy** [woordi] friends" skillfully speak against him, yet his eyes still "droppith to God" (Job 16:21). Wycliffe also uses it in his Prologue to 1 Corinthians to comment on the perversion of apostolic truth by either the Jewish sects or "the **wordy** eloquence of philosophy."

An Old Englishing of the Latin adjective *verbosus* (*verbum* equals "word"), the single word **wordy** was abandoned by later translators in favor of more **wordy** phrases: "full of words" (Wycliffe 1388), "my friends speak eloquently against me" (Geneva), and "my friends scorn me" (King James and Revised)—a trend that has culminated in the Age of Too Much Information. And given that information, **wordy** itself has taken on new meaning. Take, for example, this short list of things that have been described in recent newspapers as **wordy**: politicians and promises, screenplays and sidetrips, T-shirts and treatises, meditations and immigration papers, and even non**wordy** Shakespeare has been called "**Wordy** Willie." But a headline from the *San Diego Union-Tribune* says it all: "Nerdy **Wordy**, Technology and Language Result in Geek-Speak" (April 17, 2001).

WRINKLE

(noun) a crease or ridge caused by folding or contraction

After centuries of transformation, the Bible is now almost **wrinkle**-free. Only two lines remain where the word appears— one in Job and the other in Ephesians—and neither one is the original coinage. That distinction belongs to a 1420 Wycliffite version of Genesis, where Tamar, Judah's daughter-in-law, dons "a roket cloth with many **wrinkles** [wrynclis]" (Genesis 38:14). That usage, however, never reappears in any subsequent translation of the Bible. But the word shows up again about a hundred years later when Tyndale uses it (for the first time without a reference to cloth) in his 1526 translation of Ephesians: "a glorious congregation without spot or **wrinkle**" (Ephesians 5:27). True to the old sayings that "An old **wrinkle** never wears out" and "Religion cannot stay **wrinkles**," in recent years *Without Spot or **Wrinkle*** has been the title of several church-related books.

The noun is probably a back-formation of *wrinclod*, which is the past participle of the verb *wrinclian* ("to wind about"), also the source of the verb *to wring*. Whereas Wycliffe relies on his Old English roots, Tyndale, by contrast, translates literally from Jerome's Latin. The verb form, incidentally, appears in written English about the same time as Tyndale's use of the noun.

These days the "beauty myth" mentality has given this Old English word a new face-lift (although Montaigne's maxim that "Old age plants more **wrinkles** in the mind than in the face" ["Of Repentance," c. 1585] is probably truer than ever). Current book titles, advertisements, and treatment centers number in the thousands, all claiming to have "The **Wrinkle** Cure" or "The Daily Five-Minute Program for a Beautiful **Wrinkle**-Free Face." When Madeleine L'Engle added her own **wrinkle** to this situation by winning the 1963 Newbery Medal for her children's book *A **Wrinkle** in Time*, it was a godsend.

Υ

YE OF LITTLE FAITH

those who doubt or require more belief

As a great storm arises on the sea, the disciples become fearful of dying in a shipwreck. Aboard the ship with them, Jesus asks, "Why are ye fearful, O **ye of little faith**?" (Matthew 8:26). He calms the storm, the ship is saved, and Wycliffe adds another coinage to the English language. Later in that same story, when Peter sees Jesus walk on water, Peter tries to follow and begins to sink; when Jesus reaches out to catch the floundering disciple, he demands of Peter, "O thou of little faith, wherefore didst thou doubt?" (Matthew 14:31). Nowadays the plural form *ye* has won out over its singular pronoun form, *thou*. (In the former verse Jesus is addressing *all* disciples, but in the latter he's speaking only to Peter.)

Aimed primarily at those who are seen to be in need of stronger belief, the phrase does not apply only to religion. As the physicist Max Planck wrote in *Where Is Science Going?* (1932), "Anybody who has been seriously engaged in scientific work of any kind realizes that over the entrance to the gates of the temple of science are written the words 'Ye must have faith.' It is a quality which the scientist cannot dispense with."

Today, however, the phrase is even employed for luring new con men into business. In the 2001 Tony Award–winning musical *The Producers* by Mel Brooks and Tom Meehan, Max Bialystock urges Leo Bloom into a plan to bilk money from Broadway investors. "Oh **ye of little faith**," Max tells the reluctant Leo, inducing him into the scheme by singing "We Can Do It." (The script reads "Oh," not "O.")

The nonbelievers can be sports fans as well. An article in the *Chicago Sun-Times* underscored the "last-minute heroics which gave the Bears their sixth consecutive victory [over the Cleveland Browns]." The story opened with "O **ye of little faith**" (November 5, 2001).

Z

ZEAL

(noun) intense enthusiasm or devotion; passionate fervor

Zealotry pervades the Bible, but the word itself never appears there. Instead, both the root noun, **zeal**, and its adjective form, **zealous**, take up the cause by being first-time biblical coinages. (**Zealot** turns up a hundred years before **zeal**, and **zealotry** almost three hundred years after.) **Zeal** debuts in Wycliffe's 1382 version of 2 Kings, when Isaiah speaks the truth of the Lord to the power of Hezekiah: "The **zeal** [zeel] of the Lord of hosts," he says, shall send forth a band of survivors out of Jerusalem (2 Kings 19:31). And **zealous** makes its first appearance in Coverdale's version of 1 Kings: Elijah has taken shelter in a cave on Mount Horeb, when an "Angel of the Lord" appears to him and asks why he is there. He answers, "I have been **zealous** [zelous] for the Lord God" (1 Kings 19:10).

From a literal borrowing of the Latin noun *zelus*, and its Greek precursor, *zelos*, the common thread of "ardent feeling" carried over into English, where it also accumulated additional layers of meaning that tended to suggest the partisan aspects of rivalry and fanaticism. An old proverb reminds us that "**Zeal** is fit only for wise men, but is found mostly in fools."

Zealous? There's an English epitaph, "On a Puritanical Locksmith," that was included in a seventeenth-century collection of "Britannia":

A **zealous** locksmith died of late,
And did arrive at heaven gate,
He stood without and would not knock,
Because he meant to pick the lock.

APPENDIX ONE

A BRIEF CHRONOLOGY OF
ENGLISH TRANSLATIONS OF THE BIBLE

Before Gutenberg's invention of movable type and the printing press, the Bible (or parts of it) was reproduced by scribes who copied the text by hand. These transcriptions were called *manuscripts* (*manus* is Latin for "hand").

Year
(A.D.)

405	The earliest authorized complete Roman Catholic Bible. Translated from the Hebrew and Greek into Latin by St. Jerome, it is referred to as the Latin Vulgate.
c. 1250	Bible de St. Louis (earliest translation of the Vulgate into vernacular French).
1382	Wycliffe's Bible (earliest English translation of most of the Vulgate).
1384	Wycliffe dies.
1388	Revision of Wycliffe's 1382 version (probably by John Purvey). Completed c. 1397. The *OED* refers to 1382 and 1388 as manuscript dates. More than one hundred variations of the original manuscript appeared after the second version.

1456	Gutenberg prints Jerome's Latin version of the Bible (first typeset Bible).
1509	Henry VIII becomes king of England (dies in 1547).
1516	Erasmus makes a new Greek translation of the New Testament (NT) and corrects the Latin of the Vulgate.
1522	Luther's German translation of the NT (from Erasmus's Greek).
1523	Luther's Pentateuch, the first five books of the Old Testament (OT), from the Hebrew; Lefevre d'Etaples's French translation of the NT from the Vulgate (OT, 1528).
1524	Luther's German translation of the historical and poetical books of the OT (from the Hebrew).
1525–26	Tyndale's English NT (first complete typeset NT in English) from Erasmus's Greek and Luther's German.
1530	Tyndale's English Pentateuch and Jonah (earliest translation of Hebrew into English).
1534	Luther's complete Bible; Revised Version of Tyndale's New Testament.
1535	Coverdale's Bible (first complete English Bible) from Tyndale, Erasmus, Luther, and other extant translations. Pierre-Robert's (aka Oliveton) French translation of the complete Bible (first French Protestant Bible).
1536	Tyndale executed for heresy.

1537	Matthew's Bible (a combination of Tyndale and Coverdale by John Rogers, aka Thomas Matthew).
1539	The Great Bible (Coverdale's reworking of Matthew's Bible; the first version authorized by Henry VIII to be used in every English-speaking church).
1559	Elizabeth I becomes queen of England (dies 1603).
1560	The Geneva Bible (never authorized but portable format made it popular as the household Bible—used by Shakespeare and Puritans).
1568	The Bishop's Bible (revised in 1572 and ordered to be used in every Anglican cathedral).
1582	Rheims NT (Catholic Version of the English Bible) from the Vulgate by Roman Catholic scholars.
1603	James I becomes king of England (dies 1625).
1609	Douai OT (completes the Roman Catholic Version of the English Bible) from the Vulgate.
1611	Authorized (King James) Version published (KJ).
1881	Revised Version of King James NT.
1885	Revised Version of King James OT.
1895	Revised Version of KJ Apocrypha.
1901	American Standard KJ Version.
1946	Revised Standard KJ Version of NT.
1952	Revised Standard KJ Version of OT.
1957	Revised Standard Version of KJ Apocrypha.

APPENDIX TWO

BOOKS OF THE OLD AND NEW TESTAMENT AND
THE APOCRYPHA IN THE ORDER THEY APPEAR
IN THE KING JAMES VERSION OF THE BIBLE

Old Testament

Genesis
Exodus
Leviticus
Numbers
Deuteronomy
Joshua
Judges
Ruth
1 Samuel
2 Samuel
1 Kings
2 Kings
1 Chronicles
2 Chronicles
Ezra
Nehemiah
Esther
Job
Psalms
Proverbs

Ecclesiastes
Song of Solomon
Isaiah
Jeremiah
Lamentations
Ezekiel
Daniel
Hosea
Joel
Amos
Obadiah
Jonah
Micah
Nahum
Habakkuk
Zephaniah
Haggai
Zechariah
Malachi

Apocrypha

1 Esdras

2 Esdras

Tobit

Judith

The Rest of Esther

Wisdom

Ecclesiasticus

Baruch, with Epistle
  of Jeremiah

Song of the Three Children

The Story of Susanna

The Idol Bel, and the Dragon

The Prayer of Manasses

1 Maccabees

2 Maccabees

New Testament

Matthew

Mark

Luke

John

Acts

Romans

1 Corinthians

2 Corinthians

Galatians

Ephesians

Philippians

Colossians

1 Thessalonians

2 Thessalonians

1 Timothy

2 Timothy

Titus

Philemon

Hebrews

James

1 Peter

2 Peter

1 John

2 John

3 John

Jude

Revelation

BIBLIOGRAPHY

Allen, Ward, ed. and trans. *Translating for King James: Notes Made by a Translator of the King James Bible*. Nashville, Tenn.: Vanderbilt University Press, 1969.

Barzun, Jacques. *From Dawn to Decadence: 1500 to the Present*. New York: HarperCollins, 2000.

Baugh, Albert. *A History of the English Language*. 2nd ed. New York: Appleton-Century, 1957.

Bobrick, Benson. *Wide as the Waters: The Story of the English Bible and the Revolution It Inspired*. New York: Simon & Schuster, 2001.

Bridges, Ronald, and Luther A. Weigle. *The Bible Word Book*. New York: T. Nelson & Sons, 1960.

Butterworth, Charles C. *The Literary Lineage of the King James Bible: 1340–1611*. Philadelphia: University of Pennsylvania Press, 1941.

Buttrick, G. A., et al., eds. *The Interpreter's Dictionary of the Bible*. 4 vols. New York: Abingdon Press, 1962.

Carroll, Robert, and Stephen Prickett, eds. *The Bible: The Authorized King James Version with Apocrypha*. Oxford: Oxford University Press, 1997.

Coggan, Donald. *The English Bible*. London: Longmans, Green & Co., 1963.

Eiselen, Frederick Carl, Edwin Lewis, and David G. Downey, eds. *The Abingdon Bible Commentary*. New York: Abingdon Press, 1929.

Frye, Northrop. *The Great Code: The Bible and Literature*. New York: Harcourt Brace Jovanovich, 1982.

Goodspeed, Edgar J., ed. *The Translators to the Reader: Preface to the King James Version of 1611*. Chicago: University of Chicago Press, 1935.

Grant, Frederick C. *Translating the Bible*. Greenwich, Conn.: Seabury Press, 1961.

Hendin, David. *Guide to Biblical Coins*. 4th ed. Nyack, N.Y.: Amphora Books, 2001.

McGrath, Alister. *In the Beginning: The Story of the King James Bible and How It Changed a Nation, a Language, and a Culture*. New York: Doubleday, 2001.

Miller, Madeleine S., and J. Lane. *The New Harper's Bible Dictionary*. New York: Harper & Row, 1973.

Norton, David. *A History of the English Bible as Literature*. Cambridge, U.K.: Cambridge University Press, 2000. Originally published in 2 vols. in 1993.

Prickett, Stephen. *Words and* The Word: *Language, Poetics and Biblical Interpretation*. Cambridge, U.K.: Cambridge University Press, 1986.

Richards, Lawrence O. *The New International Encyclopedia of Bible Words*. Grand Rapids, Mich.: Zondervan, 1991.

Safire, William. *Safire's New Political Dictionary*. New York: Random House, 1993.

Strong, James. *The Exhaustive Concordance of the Bible*. Peabody, Mass.: Hendrickson Publishers, 1992. Originally published in 1890.

Tyndale, William, trans. *Tyndale's New Testament*. Introduction and Modern Spelling Edition by David Daniell. New Haven, Conn.: Yale University Press, 1989.

————, trans. *Tyndale's Old Testament: Being the Pentateuch of 1530, Joshua to 2 Chronicles of 1537, and Jonah*. Introduction and Modern Spelling Edition by David Daniell. New Haven, Conn.: Yale University Press, 1992.

Westcott, Brooke F. *History of the English Bible*. Reprint of 1905, 3rd ed. Eugene, Ore.: Wipf and Stock, 1998. Originally published in 1868.

Whittingham, William, ed. *Geneva Bible*. Cincinnati, Ohio: Lazarus Ministry Press, 1998. First printed in Geneva, Switzerland, in 1560.

Wilson, Derek. *The People & the Book*. London: Barrie & Jenkins, Ltd., 1976.

Wycliffe, John, and His Followers. *The Holy Bible, Containing the Old and New Testaments*. 4 vols. Edited by Josiah Forshall and Frederic Madden. (Reprint of 1850 edition. Oxford: Oxford University Press, 1850.) New York: AMS Press, 1982.

INDEX
BY ENGLISH TRANSLATIONS
OF THE BIBLE

graven image (Exodus 20:4)
handmaid (Psalms 122:2)
horror (Deuteronomy 32:10)
interpret (Daniel 5:16)
interpretation (Daniel 5:14) (in
    interpret)
irrevocable (Ezekiel 21:5)
ivory tower (Song of Solomon
    7:4)
keys of the kingdom (Matthew
    16:19)
legacy (2 Corinthians 5:20)
liberty (2 Corinthians 3:17)
liquid (Ezekiel 44:30)
ministry (Ezekiel 44:13 and
    Colossians 4:17)
mutter (2 Samuel 12:19)
mystery (Daniel 2:27 and
    Romans 16:25)
needlework (Exodus 26:1)
novelty (1 Timothy 6:20)
offend (James 3:2)
offense (Philippians 1:10) (in
    offend)
persuasion (Galatians 5:8)
plague (Revelation 9:18)
problem (Judges 14:15)
puberty (Malachi 2:14)
quick and the dead (1 Peter 4:5)
quiet (1 Thessalonians 4:11)
reap the whirlwind (Hosea 8:7)
root of all evil (1 Timothy 6:10)

salt of the earth (Matthew 5:13)
scrape (Job 2:8)
seer (1 Kings 9:9)
sex (Genesis 6:19)
shibboleth (Judges 12:6)
Sodom and Gomorrah (Genesis
    13:10)
transfer (Ezekiel 48:14)
treasure (Isaiah 39:6)
uncertainty (1 Timothy 6:17)
under the sun (Ecclesiastes 1:9)
voice of the turtle (Song of
    Solomon 2:12)
wordy (Job 16:21)
wrinkle (Genesis 38:14) (1420)
ye of little faith (Matthew 8:26)
zeal (2 Kings 19:31)

TYNDALE (1525–26 AND
1530/34)
alpha and omega (Revelation
    1:19)
apple of his eye (Deuteronomy
    32:10)
beautiful (Matthew 23:27)
blind lead the blind (Matthew
    15:14)
brokenhearted (Luke 4:18)
brother's keeper (Genesis 4:9)
busybody (1 Peter 4:15)
castaway (1 Corinthians 9:27
    and 2 Corinthians 13:5)

cast the first stone (John 8:7)

coat of many colors (Genesis 37:3)

eat, drink, and be merry (Ecclesiastes 8:15)

fisherman (Luke 5:2)

full of days (Genesis 35:29)

housetop (Matthew 24:17)

infidel (2 Corinthians 6:15 and 1 Timothy 5:8)

Jehovah (Exodus 6:3)

judge not (Matthew 7:1)

land of Nod (Genesis 4:16)

no man can serve two masters (Matthew 6:24)

nurse (Exodus 2:9)

Passover (Exodus 12:11)

pillar of salt (Genesis 19:26)

rose-colored (Revelation 17:3)

scapegoat (Leviticus 16:8)

seashore (Hebrews 11:12)

seventy times seven (Matthew 18:22)

sin of the fathers (Exodus 20:5)

sorcerer (Acts 13:6)

stiff-necked (Acts 7:51)

stranger in a strange land (Exodus 2:22)

suffer fools gladly (2 Corinthians 11:19)

thirty pieces of silver (Matthew 26:14)

two-edged sword (Hebrews 4:12)

undergird (Acts 27:17)

ungodly (Romans 5:6)

uproar (Acts 21:38)

viper (Matthew 3:7 and Acts 28:3)

COVERDALE (1535)

bald head (2 Kings 2:23)

blab (Proverbs 15:2)

blood money (Matthew 27:6)

bloodthirsty (Psalms 25:9) (in **blood money**)

consumer (Malachi 3:2)

daytime (Psalms 22:2)

left wing (1 Maccabees 9:16)

nursing (Isaiah 49:23) (in **nurse**)

peace offering (1 Maccabees 1:45)

slaughter (Isaiah 22:13)

sprinkler (Jeremiah 52:18)

voiceless (Acts 8:32)

zealous (1 Kings 19.10) (in **zeal**)

GENEVA (1560)

Ancient of Days (Daniel 7:9)

burnt offering (Genesis 8:20 and Genesis 22:2)

get thee behind me, Satan (Matthew 16:23)

holier than thou (Isaiah 65:5)
house divided (Matthew 12:25)
my cup runneth over (Psalms
  23:5)
network (Exodus 27:4)
stargazer (Isaiah 47:13)
through a glass darkly
  (1 Corinthians 13:12)

KING JAMES (1611)
balm in Gilead (Jeremiah 8:22)
not live by bread alone
  (Matthew 4:4)

INDEX
BY BOOKS OF THE BIBLE

Abbreviations:
W—Wycliffe (1382/88)
T—Tyndale (1525–26 & 1530/34)
C—Coverdale (1535)
G—Geneva (1560)
KJ—King James (1611)

Old Testament

GENESIS
brother's keeper (4:9 T)
burnt offering (8:20 and
 22:2 G)
childbearing (adjective)
 (25:24 W)
coat of many colors (37:3 T)
female (1:27 W)
full of days (35:29 T)
land of Nod (4:16 T)
pillar of salt (19:26 T)
sex (6:19 W)
Sodom and Gomorrah
 (13:10 W)
wrinkle (38:14 W [1420])

EXODUS
affliction (3:7 W)
eye for eye (21:24 T)
graven image (20:4 W [1388])
Jehovah (6:3 T)
needlework (26:1 W)
network (27:4 G)
nurse (2:9 T)
Passover (12:11 T)
sin of the fathers (20:5 T)
stranger in a strange land (2:22 T)

LEVITICUS
consume (16:23 W)
scapegoat (16:8 T)

NUMBERS
cast (35:17 W) (in **castaway**)
first fruits (18:12 W)

DEUTERONOMY
apple of his eye (32:10 T)
grasp (28:29 W)
horror (32:10 W)

JUDGES
problem (14:15 W)
shibboleth (12:6 W)

RUTH
affinity (3:13 W)

2 SAMUEL
mutter (12:19 W)

1 KINGS
seer (9:9 W)
zealous (19:10 C) (in **zeal**)

2 KINGS
bald head (2:23 C)
zeal (19:3 W)

2 CHRONICLES
botch (34:10 W)

JOB
scrape (2:8 W)
wordy (16:21 W)

PSALMS
bloodthirsty (25:9 C) (in **blood money**)
contradiction (54:10 W)
daytime (22:2 C)
handmaid (122:2 W)
my cup runneth over (23:5 G)

PROVERBS
blab (15:2 C)
glory (17:6 W)

ECCLESIASTES
eat, drink, and be merry (8:15 T)
under the sun (1:9 W)

SONG OF SOLOMON
bundle (1:12 W [1388])
ivory tower (7:4 W)
voice of the turtle (2:12 W)

ISAIAH
brain (66:3 W)
childbearing (noun) (49:21 W)
feel (59:10 W)
holier than thou (65:5 G)
nursing (Isaiah 49:23 C) (in **nurse**)
slaughter (22:13 C)
stargazer (47:13 G)
treasure (39:6 W)

JEREMIAH
balm in Gilead (8:22 KJ)
sprinkler (52:18 C)

EZEKIEL
appetite (21:16 W)
doubtful (12:24 W [1388])
irrevocable (21:5 W)
liquid (44:30 W)
ministry (44:13 W)
transfer (48:14 W)

DANIEL
Ancient of Days (7:9 G)
interpret (5:16 W)

interpretation (5:14 W) (in
   interpret)
mystery (2:27 W)

HOSEA
reap the whirlwind (8:7 W)

ZECHARIAH
filthy (3:3 W)

MALACHI
consumer (3:2 C)
puberty (2:14 W)

Apocrypha

BARUCH
cucumber (6:69 W)

ECCLESIASTICUS
dishonor (v) (10:23 W [1388])

1 MACCABEES
left wing (9:16 C)
peace offering (1:45 C)

New Testament

MATTHEW
beautiful (23:27 T)
blind lead the blind (15:14 T)
blood money (27:6 C)

city set on a hill (5:14 W)
doctrine (15:9 W)
get thee behind me, Satan
   (16:23 G)

house divided (12:25 G)
housetop (24:17 T)
judge not (7:1 T)
keys of the kingdom (16:19 W)
no man can serve two masters
  (6:24 T)
not live by bread alone (4:4 KJ)
salt of the earth (5:13 W)
seventy times seven (18:22 T)
thirty pieces of silver (26:14 T)
viper (3:7 T)
ye of little faith (8:26 W)

LUKE
brokenhearted (4:18 T)
fisherman (5:2 T)
glory (2:14 W)

JOHN
born again (3:3 W)
cast the first stone (8:7 T)

ACTS
argument (1:13 W)
civility (22:28 W)
common (2:44 W) (in **communication**)
crime (23:29 and 25:16 W)
ecstasy (3:10 W)
exorcist (19:13 W)
sorcerer (13:6 T)
stiff-necked (7:51 T)

undergird (27:17 T)
uproar (21:38 T)
viper (28:3 T)
voiceless (8:32 C)

ROMANS
adoption (8:23 W)
glory (1:23 W)
mystery (16:25 W)
ungodly (5:6 T)

1 CORINTHIANS
all things to all men (9:22 W)
ambitious (13:5 W)
castaway (9:27 T)
conscience (8:7 W)
excellent (12:31 W)
glory (10:31 W)
through a glass darkly (13:12 G)

2 CORINTHIANS
castaway (13:5 T)
communication (9:13 W)
conscience (5:11 W)
infidel (6:15 T)
legacy (5:20 W)
liberty (3:17 W)
suffer fools gladly (11:19 T)

GALATIANS
allegory (4:24 W)
persuasion (5:8 W)

PHILIPPIANS
offense (1:10 W) (in **offend**)

COLOSSIANS
ministry (4:17 W)

1 THESSALONIANS
quiet (4:11W)

1 TIMOTHY
infidel (5:8 T)
novelty (6:20 W)
root of all evil (6:10 W)
uncertainty (6:17 W)

HEBREWS
seashore (11:12 T)
two-edged sword (4:12 T)

JAMES
offend (3:2 W)

1 PETER
busybody (4:15 T)
conscience (2:19 W)
quick and the dead (4:5 [1388])

REVELATION
alpha and omega (1:19 T)
plague (9:18 W)
rose-colored (17:3 T)

INDEX

BY WORDS AND PHRASES

Abbreviations:
W—Wycliffe (1382/88)
T—Tyndale (1525–26 & 1530/34)
C—Coverdale (1535)
G—Geneva (1560)
KJ—King James (1611)

burnt offering (Genesis 8:20 and Genesis 22:2 G)

busybody (1 Peter 4:15 T)

C

cast (Numbers 35:17 W) (in **castaway**)

castaway (1 Corinthians 9:27 and 2 Corinthians 13:5 T)

cast the first stone (John 8:7 T)

childbearing (noun) (Isaiah 49:21 W)

childbearing (adjective) (Genesis 25:24 W)

city set on a hill (Matthew 5:14 W)

civility (Acts 22:28 W)

coat of many colors (Genesis 37:3 T)

common (Acts 2:44 W) (in **communication**)

communication (2 Corinthians 9:13 W)

conscience (1 Corinthians 8:7, 2 Corinthians 5:11, and 1 Peter 2:19 W)

consume (Leviticus 6:23 W)

consumer (Malachi 3:2 C)

contradiction (Psalms 54:10 W)

crime (Acts 23:29 and Acts 25:16 W)

cucumber (Baruch 6:69 W)

D

daytime (Psalms 22:2 C)

dishonor (Ecclesiasticus 10:23 W [1388])

doctrine (Matthew 15:9 W)

doubtful (Ezekiel 12:24 W [1388])

E

eat, drink, and be merry (Ecclesiastes 8:15 T)

ecstasy (Acts 3:10 W)

excellent (1 Corinthians 12:31 W)

exorcist (Acts 19:13 W)

eye for eye (Exodus 21:24 W)

F

feel (Isaiah 59:10 W)

female (Genesis 1:27 W)

filthy (Zechariah 3:3 W)

first fruits (Numbers 18:12 W)

fisherman (Luke 5:2 T)

full of days (Genesis 35:29 T)

G

get thee behind me, Satan (Matthew 16:23 G)

glory (Proverbs 17:6, Luke 2:14, Romans 1:23, and 1 Corinthians 10:31 W)

grasp (Deuteronomy 28:29 W)

graven image (Exodus 20:4 W
   [1388])

H

handmaid (Psalms 122:2 W)
holier than thou (Isaiah 65:5 G)
horror (Deuteronomy 32:10 W)
house divided (Matthew
   12:25 G)
housetop (Matthew 24:17 T)

I

infidel (2 Corinthians 6:15 and
   1 Timothy 5:8 T)
interpret (Daniel 5:16 W)
interpretation (Daniel 5:14 W)
   (in **interpret**)
irrevocable (Ezekiel 21:5 W)
ivory tower (Song of Solomon
   7:4 W)

J

Jehovah (Exodus 6:3 T)
judge not (Matthew 7:1 T)

K

keys of the kingdom (Matthew
   16:19 W)

L

land of Nod (Genesis 4:16 T)
left wing (1 Maccabees 9:16 C)

legacy (2 Corinthians 5:20 W)
liberty (2 Corinthians 3:17 W)
liquid (Ezekiel 44:30 W)

M

ministry (Ezekiel 44:13 and
   Colossians 4:17 W)
mutter (2 Samuel 12:19 W)
my cup runneth over (Psalms
   23:5 G)
mystery (Daniel 2:27 and
   Romans 16:25 W)

N

needlework (Exodus 26:1 W)
network (Exodus 27:4 G)
no man can serve two masters
   (Matthew 6:24 T)
not live by bread alone
   (Matthew 4:4 KJ)
novelty (1 Timothy 6:20 W)
nurse (Exodus 2:9 T)
nursing (Isaiah 49:23 C) (in
   nurse)

O

offend (James 3:2 W)
offense (Philippians 1:10 W) (in
   offend)

P

Passover (Exodus 12:11 T)

peace offering (1 Maccabees 1:45 C)

persuasion (Galatians 5:8 W)

pillar of salt (Genesis 19:26 T)

plague (Revelation 9:18)

problem (Judges 14:15 W)

puberty (Malachi 2:14 W)

Q

quick and the dead (1 Peter 4:5 W [1388])

quiet (1 Thessalonians 4:11 W)

R

reap the whirlwind (Hosea 8:7 W)

root of all evil (1 Timothy 6:10 W)

rose-colored (Revelation 17:3 T)

S

salt of the earth (Matthew 5:13 W)

scapegoat (Leviticus 16:8 T)

scrape (Job 2:8 W)

seashore (Hebrews 11:12 T)

seer (1 Kings 9:9 W)

seventy times seven (Matthew 18:22 T)

sex (Genesis 6:19 W)

shibboleth (Judges 12:6 W)

sin of the fathers (Exodus 20:5 T)

slaughter (Isaiah 22:13 C)

Sodom and Gomorrah (Genesis 13:10 W)

sorcerer (Acts 13:6 T)

sprinkler (Jeremiah 52:18 C)

stargazer (Isaiah 47:13 G)

stiff-necked (Acts 7:51 T)

stranger in a strange land (Exodus 2:22 T)

suffer fools gladly (2 Corinthians 11:19 T)

T

thirty pieces of silver (Matthew 26:14 T)

through a glass darkly (1 Corinthians 13:12 G)

transfer (Ezekiel 48:14 W)

treasure (Isaiah 39:6 W)

two-edged sword (Hebrews 4:12 T)

U

uncertainty (1 Timothy 6:17 W)

undergird (Acts 27:17 T)

under the sun (Ecclesiastes 1:9 W)

ungodly (Romans 5:6 T)

uproar (Acts 21:38 T)

V

viper (Matthew 3:7 and Acts
28:3 T)
voiceless (Acts 8:32 C)
voice of the turtle (Song of
Solomon 2:12 W)

W

wordy (Job 16:21 W)
wrinkle (Genesis 38:14 W
[1420])

Y

ye of little faith (Matthew
8:26 W)

Z

zeal (2 Kings 19:31 W)
zealous (1 Kings 19:10 C) (in
zeal)

ABOUT THE AUTHORS

Stanley Malless is an associate professor of education at Simpson College in Indianola, Iowa, where he teaches courses in history, philosophy, and psychology of education. He holds undergraduate degrees in English and French, an M.A. in six-teenth- and seventeenth-century British literature, and a Ph.D. in education. He is the coauthor of *The Elements of English* and *Coined by Shakespeare*.

Jeffrey McQuain is the author of *Power Language* and *Never Enough Words*, and the coauthor of *The Elements of English* and *Coined by Shakespeare*. For fourteen years he served as the researcher for William Safire's "On Language" column in the *New York Times Magazine* and most recently has been the edi-tor of the newsletter *Copy Editor*. He has also written an inter-nationally syndicated column about words. Dr. McQuain holds a Ph.D. in literary studies from American University in Washington, D.C., and lives in Potomac, Maryland.